EBONY ISLAND

LINDA HOLZ

ISBN: 979-8-88945-017-7
eISBN: 979-8-88945-018-4

Brilliant Books Literary
137 Forest Park Lane Thomasville
North Carolina 27360 USA

Printed in the United States of America

CONTENTS

PREFACE

After watching the third Jurassic Park movie, especially with the scene where the raptors confronted the people for the return of their eggs a thought occurred. The raptors were so caring for the eggs. What would it be like after they were hatched? This idea sat for a while when another thought happened. What would it be like if the people and the raptors worked together for a common purpose? From this idea I went with the thought of a mother's love, hence the sub-title of the story for each part and the central theme throughout the book.

The love a mother has for their young can be expressed in many different ways. Some humans and animals have been known to neglect the care of their young. While on the other hand there are those people, as well as animals who will go to such an extreme level to protect or save their young ones from harm, even with the potential of sacrificing their own lives. Even though people know the quality of love animals do not but that does not mean they can't express it by their actions. A mother's protecting and nurturing instincts can be very strong.

In the second part I went a step farther and centered on the next subject a mother centers her life on—the father of her child. The man in a women's life can be the most pivotal part to holding her family together. To what lengths would she go to keep him safe?

The third part centers on the same manner as the second with the roles reversed.

I also went on the precept that the raptors were clever and smart even though most of the studies conducted steer in the other direction. As in any fiction material there is always the author's opinion and this is mine, as what I think it would have been like if the raptors possessed intelligence. I hope you enjoy reading it as I had in writing it!

RAPTOR TERMS

Two-legger –   people

Speed Creatures –   any motorized vehicle

Cavern –   an open airplane or building

Trail –   ramp

"The bravest are the tenderest,
The loving are the daring."

Alice Stone Blackwell
Dorchester, Mass., June 3, 1909

PART ONE

A MOTHER'S LOVE FOR THAT OF A CHILD

Concealed by the ferns and trees along the forests edge the mother raptor watched the fishing boat move parallel with the beach as it maneuvered around the rocks, careful not to get too close. At least once a week the vessel made the journey. A soft warm breeze blew through the ferns, bringing the tantalizing aroma of fish to tease the senses of the mother raptor, mixed with another familiar scent, the two-leggers. She remembered them from years ago when they had stolen eggs from the nests and their rather agile ability to climb.

A sudden movement from the fishing boat caught her attention resulting in her emitting a purring sound from deep in her throat and blinking in anticipation. One of the two-leggers stood at the vessels edge, holding a container, of which he quickly dumped over the side. The mother raptor watched some of the contents sink out of sight as others floated on the tide, toward the beach. A few minutes later the mother raptor moved from her place of concealment, confident that it was safe as the fishing vessel moved out of sight. She walked over to the objects the tide had left in the sand. Picking up a couple of them she quickly moved to the forests edge, knowing full well the dangers of staying out in the open for long. When with her pack she was nearly invincible, but alone she could easily be picked off by a T-rex or other predator.

Setting the objects down on a smooth patch of grass she looked closely at them. They were not edible, that was obvious, but the images displayed on them intrigued her. One contained a two-legger sitting on a strange looking creature with four legs, long flowing tail and mane. A different one showed a very small two-legger being held by a larger one. Another male stood close beside them. Both were smiling at the small two-legger. Another image from the second object showed a two-legger climbing up a stone-faced cliff. She looked at them a moment longer when a sudden noise shifted her attention. She recognized it immediately as coming from one of her pack and responded back, while searching the forest for movement. Shortly her mate, the alpha male appeared. They greeted each other by sniffing, nipping, and rubbing their bodies to affirm their identities and relationship. Once done they turned in the direction of the nesting site, leaving the two magazines behind.

＊ ＊ ＊ ＊ ＊

Laura Matthews Sinclair reached into the box, extracting the tiny striped bundle of fur. Holding him close with one hand she reached for the bottle filled with a milk type formula sitting on a nearby counter. Placing the nipple into the little one's mouth she watched the tiger cub gulp down the creamy liquid. When done Laura repeated the process with the sibling. It was sad that the mother had abandoned them but fortunate that she and the rest of the staff were able to take over. Since she had taken this job as the zoo's veterinarian she never regretted a single moment. She loved working with animals. The only downside was her obnoxious boss. Even though she was one of many veterinarians at the San Diego Zoo her boss seemed to pay the most attention to her, especially before she got married. His attempts at flirting or asking her out just turned her stomach. Even though the man was attractive to look at she sensed a side of him she did not want to know.

Once the tiger cubs were fed she handed them over to an attendant just in time to see her husband walking toward her. She smiled a greeting as she thought; 'Now there is a handsome man!' Running into his arms she gave him a passionate kiss, anxious to tell him the good news she had learned earlier in the day.

* * * * *

The mother raptor watched the hatchlings as they moved about in the nest. Only two days old and they were able to eat regurgitated meat easily, even though they were no bigger than a small chicken. With the event of their entry into the world tension was high in seeing to their safety. Even though the nests were in a secure area there was still the possible discovery by a scavenger or predator. All were on the alert for danger. Only a select few would leave when time to hunt.

As the mother raptor watched the young in their playful antics she was unaware of a pair of eyes watching. Down wind of the nests and concealed from site was an Elmisaurus. Even though he usually preyed on small mammals and insects he would not be one to pass up an opportunity to snatch a hatchling from an unguarded nest. He felt confident in his abilities as a speedy predator and waited patiently for the right moment, which happened sooner than he expected. The raptors were moving out to hunt leaving the mother raptor and four others to guard the three nests. The alpha male was leading the hunt.

Soon after the pack had left, an intruder happened onto the nesting sight. A hapless plant eater, wandering from his herd in search of tasty green ferns found him-self face-to-face with the raptors. The raptors took immediate action placing themselves between the plant eater and the nests they stood their ground. They could have easily taken the plant eater but chose not to, their main objective was to protect the nests. In its state of panic the animal could easily trample the hatchlings. By placing themselves where they did the five raptors guided the plant eater in one direction, back the way it had come. At the moment the animal turned to leave the Elmisaurus moved from its hiding spot. Running up to the closest nest he used his flexible hands and grabbed one of the hatchlings. Turning the Elmisaurus quickly sprinted away on his two nimble legs. The mother raptor caught the sudden movement and turned in time to see the retreating form of the Elmisaurus and hear the distress call of her young.

Even though the Elmisaurus was a speedy moving predator the raptors had long muscular legs built for speed and the mother raptor quickly took advantage of her own by releasing an alarm call and giving chase, two other raptors following her lead. The Elmisaurus ran over the forest floor, dodging bushes and trees before breaking through into a small clearing. Sprinting to the other side he suddenly stopped. He could go no farther as he now faced a deep precipice. He turned to change direction and stopped again as the three raptors walked slowly toward him. The Elmisaurus stepped back, forgetting what was behind him. When the ground began to shift and move he realized his mistake. The ground gave way at that moment and he fell, taking the hatchling with him. The raptors screeched in alarm, running up to the cliff's edge. Careful not to step near the area the Elmisaurus disappeared they searched for their hatchling. As the dust cleared they saw the Elmisaurus lying on its side. It had fared badly having broken its back and neck while landing partially in a newly abandoned Pteranodon nest. A movement within the nest revealed the hatchling, having landed in soft ferns and other vegetation, unharmed.

The mother raptor called to the hatchling and it answered in kind as the two other raptors looked at their alpha female for guidance. They were soon joined by several others including the alpha male, having returned from a successful hunt. Treating the hatchling as though it were in its own nest one Raptor regurgitated a meal over the edge allowing it to land on top of the dead Elmisaurus and spread into a small portion of the nest so the hatchling could eat. All the while the mother raptor realized this was a problem. The hatchling could not get off the ledge nor could they reach it. Her mind searched for an answer, looking around her for a solution. When she saw a tree and remembered the two-leggers climbing them, followed by the images on the beach, she knew what needed to be done.

Turning to her alpha male she nudged him while making several clicking sounds. He understood by returning the gesture. With that the mother raptor turned and ran back into the forest.

* * * * *

"Are you serious?" Bradley Sinclair questioned as he looked at the flushed features of his wife's face and gazed into her soft hazel eyes, alert and sparkling with life; as if searching for final confirmation.

"Yes I am serious! I'm three and a half months pregnant. We are going to have a baby!"

Bradley hugged his wife close to him, elated beyond measure. Even now, two days later, as he relived the moment he was still awestruck. He was going to be a father! As he parked the car in their two stall garage the previous thoughts were replaced with a little girl having the same beautiful features of his wife, a miniature version but with her own distinct personality. Reaching for the bouquet of yellow roses he left the car to search for his wife, although he had a general idea where she would be in their two story house at this time of the day. As he moved through the butler's pantry he quickly glanced into the kitchen, smiling a greeting to Rosa their housekeeper, maid, and cook all rolled into one as she put the final touches to their evening meal. Rosa just smiled back and shook her head as Bradley disappeared, entering the stairway. She knew what was making that man so happy.

Bradley guessed correctly as he entered what once had been an extra bedroom but was now converted into their computer room and office combined. There were two other bedrooms besides the master, of which the one closest to the master bedroom would become the nursery. Laura was sitting in front of her computer researching her favorite topic, dinosaurs, with the main category being Velociraptors.

"Hard at work I see," spoke Bradley as he reached down to give her a kiss on the forehead.

"Oh, hi. Yes and getting quite frustrated. So far all I have found on this animal is what people think it might be. One says they are less intelligent than modern big cats. Even lower than that, one compares them to an ostrich or chicken. Then there are reports from the Paleontologist, Dr. Grant who refers to them being as smart as dolphins, or primates, and reports seeing them open a door. Then there were those who were on Isla Angusti Don who witnessed raptors deliberately setting them up to trick them. Other descriptions say they are cunning and clever. I know there has to be more to this species and I would love to travel to Isla Angusti Don to study them."

"I can understand how you feel Laura, but that is impossible. You know how deadly these animals are, not to mention the fact that the island is now a dinosaur reserve. No one is to disturb the island or the prehistoric wildlife. They even changed the name to discourage others from getting curious and checking it out. It stands for island of sharp teeth. So far the name change has worked."

Laura sighed, "Yes, I know, but there is always a chance that things may change."

"That's my wife, always the optimist." Bradley took that moment to hand her the bouquet of roses, and watching her face light up was the best medicine for him. "Why don't we put these in water and get a bite to eat. I am sure that Rosa has supper ready."

* * * * *

Day 1 later part

The mother raptor once again watched the fishing boat from her place of concealment, although this time her vantage point was located a bit farther up than before. Below her was another small stretch of beach covered sporadically with small rocks. Beyond that the rocks grew to form boulders and rock formations extending above the water's surface. To outsiders it was known as Ancient Rock even though there was more than one. To the mother raptor it was her path to the boat. As dusk settled, giving the promise of eventual darkness she left her place of concealment, raced across the beach, and leapt from one boulder to the next. When she reached the last boulder she froze and waited, ignoring the sea mist spraying around her from the waves. As the boat came abreast of her position she made the final leap, landing on the deck near the back of the vessel. Grateful that the boat was larger than most other fishing boats and built for longer distances in offering her a place to hide, she quickly ducked into the cold, quiet and dark hold of the boat. Her landing did cause a slight bump to the vessel, resulting in the crew's investigation. By the time they arrived on deck the mother raptor was safely ensconced in the dark interior, surrounded by the ever present odor of fish. She would not grow hungry on this trip.

Five hours later the vessel pulled into the port of Ciudad Cortes for supplies. The mother raptor slept after gorging herself on a meal of fish, oblivious to the commotion above. Soon the boat was off again, this time following the Sierpe River to dock once again in Palmar Sur, the final stop to delivering their cargo.

Since it was well into the night the men decided to visit one of the riverside restaurants, confident that one would be open at such a late hour. After that a few hours of sleep were on the agenda, in one of the hotels. An hour after they left the mother raptor woke up hungry, and cold. Since the hold was kept in a chilled condition to keep the fish preserved she was not use to such temperatures, which caused her to move sluggishly. After quickly eating some more fish she left the hold and, arriving on the deck, found it to be abandoned. Now she was confronted with a new challenge. Everything looked foreign to her as she gazed past the fishing boat to the town of Palmar Sur. Remembering her goal of searching for a specific two-legger, confident that she was following the right trail, she left the boat to explore, slowly at first as her limbs started to warm up.

When morning came the men returned to their boat, ready to unload its contents. Entering the hold they were met with a huge surprise. Only a very small pile of fish was left intermixed with scattered remnants of partially eaten ones. They were dumb-founded as to what could have gotten into their cargo hold. It did not take them long to figure it out when one of them found evidence of the animals passing. Still finding it difficult to ascertain the animal's identity they agreed on one specific thing: the animal was a meat eater and the town should be notified. Once again they left the boat to do just that, confident in the knowledge that they at least had two loads safely on the cargo plane. Two out of three wasn't bad.

Day 2 eight hours later

By the time the men left the vessel the mother raptor had traveled through the main plaza and past a little church in the center of town to find her-self facing an open stretch of ground containing all manner of strange things. In the mix, of course were two-leggers. Staying out of sight as much as possible she maneuvered herself to observe the two-leggers. As she watched the beginning pangs of hunger set in. These two-leggers were not what she searched for but she also remembered they were quite edible. As one of them separated from the others and moving close to her vantage point she crunched down to spring. It was at that time the wind changed direction and a familiar scent reached her. Turning her head toward the scent her eyes set on a dark huge cavern above her and a small trail leading inside. She looked again at the two-legger in time to see him disappear inside another smaller cavern made of wood. Looking around again she noted others but they were far away. Some were in speed creatures, moving from one place to another, while others carried boxes, and crates. Quickly leaving her hiding place the mother raptor jumped on the short trail and soon disappeared into the dark interior of the cavern. Once inside she took in her surroundings. Moving toward one of the crates she detected the distinct odor of fish, even though the smell was prominent throughout.

At that moment the mother raptor turned to face the loud sound descending on her from behind. A speed creature carrying a crate came up the ramp and straight at her. Turning abruptly to face the challenge, which caused her tail to whip around, hitting another crate, cracking and splintering the wood, she hissed loudly. Stepping back briefly she turned again and darted behind some stacked crates, just as the driver of the fork lift paused, thinking there was something wrong with his machine. Not hearing anything more he shrugged his shoulders and finished his task. Shortly after he exited, the ramp was removed, and the door closed.

The Boeing 767 freighter started its engines to prepare for take off. Being fourth in a series of seven the cargo plane had been converted from passenger to freighter by a Japanese airline industry called ANA. The goal was to strengthen and expand ANA's cargo business so the aircraft would be used where the demand was highest. At this time the demand came for the delivery of fish, so the Costa Rican government arranged to expand their runway in Palmar Sur to accommodate the freighter's size, then contacting ANA to make the arrangements. This type of fish was in high demand by quite a few restaurants worldwide so the government was looking for an aircraft to give faster deliveries with fewer stops. ANA's Board of Directors was quite willing to prove that they were the one for the job. So it was that the ANA Cargo freighter traveled down the runway of Palmar Sur's airport to lift off in the direction of its first delivery, the San Diego International Airport, California.

Day 2 mid morning

The mother Raptor stayed hidden until the freighter had gained altitude and leveled out. Since she was alone she knew to be more cautious. The noises were strange and foreign to her but she soon adapted to her new surroundings. The crate she had cracked and splintered was easily expanded by using her claw, offering her an abundant supply of food. Her only problem, which offered some discomfort, was the cool temperature, and that her food was kept on ice. Even though she had attempted to drink water earlier what she needed most was the nourishment that a fresh kill would give her. For now, she had to make do with what she had and ate the fish until full. Afterwards she found a pile of tarp to lie down and rest. Several hours later she was back up again to eat and explore, her movements being somewhat slow.

* * * * *

The pilot of the ANA Cargo, Ben Hayato yawned sleepily as he rechecked the instrument panel, especially the flight and engine instruments to see that all was working properly. He glanced over to his co-pilot, Mitch, and noted that he was also checking things over. Looking back to the panel he glanced at the GPS, auto pilot, and temperature gauges. All looked good. The cool temperature in back was still being maintained and since the plane was now in auto pilot they could relax a little. Mitch, on the other hand, had other ideas.

"Well if you don't mind Ben, I am going to the can. Sure you can handle it while I am gone?"

Ben gave him a look that said, 'are you kidding.' Mitch smiled and rose from his seat. Walking through the narrow archway behind them he turned to the right and opened the door to the restroom. He paused briefly to look at a calendar, which someone had hung on the side of the 9G cargo barrier that separated them from the cargo hold, although to Mitch it just looked like another wall with an access door. He smiled at the beautiful girl pictured on the top part of the calendar, then entered the small room complete with a toilet, small sink, and mirror. Once finished he washed his hands and turned to exit the room. It was at that moment that a bit of turbulence caused the plane to jump. A moment after that a crate crashed to the floor in the cargo hold.

Mitch, walking up to the doorway to face the flight deck where Ben sat winced at the sound. "Hey can you keep it level. Things are shifting back there. Something crashed for sure. I'm going to check it out."

"Okay," Ben acknowledged.

"Can you turn the lights on back there?"

"Sure, no problem." Ben reached over to the panel and flipped a switch. "Done."

Turning back Mitch walked over to the cargo door. Reaching up to his right he pushed a button on the control panel then pulled the manual latch on the door down while pushing at the same time. Being new the door opened without a sound allowing Mitch to step through. As he progressed toward the back he saw the crate that had fallen. It looked undamaged and there was no way he could pick it up due to its size. He noted the blue sticker indicating that the contents were non-breakable. The stickers came in handy since they always had more than one type of item to ship. Satisfied that it would be okay he started to turn back when movements beside a nearby crate made him stop. It was at that moment the mother raptor stepped out into full view. Mitch stood transfixed at the sight before him. When the animal screeched loudly at him did he break from his trance to turn and run. Adrenaline rushing through him Mitch did not pause or break stride. His one goal was to reach the door, which seemed so far away. His imagination getting the better of him he could almost feel the breath of the animal on the back of his neck. This induced him to have a quick burst of speed causing him to run into the door. He quickly slipped through, slamming it shut just in time to hear a thud hit on the other side. Quickly he bolted the door manually and secured it by double locking it through the control panel. He paused to take deep breaths while looking at the door. Taking a step backward his eyes grew round as he watched in horror as the door's latch moved down then up. The latch repeated the movement once more then stopped. Confident that the door would hold he moved to the front of the plane and sat in his seat in front of the control panel, taking some deep calming breaths. Ben looked over and noted his disheveled appearance.

"What happened to you? Did one of the crates attack?"

"Not exactly a crate. Why don't you turn the video camera on and look for yourself."

With a puzzled frown Ben did as suggested. Two small monitors, one located to the right of Ben, and the other to Mitch's left flashed on revealing portions of the cargo hold, and something else. Mitch then had the satisfaction of hearing Ben cuss in Japanese. The minutes ticked by as they both watched the mother raptor move about.

"How the heck did that get on our plane?"

"Good question," Mitch replied. "How long till we land?"

"A good forty-five minutes," said Ben.

"Well I think we had better radio the tower, tell them what we have here so they can prepare. It will probably take that long to convince them."

* * * * *

Laura watched her friend, Jill Garner climb a wall at the Solid Rock Climbing Gym. At least once a week the two of them went to the gym to practice their climbing skills. They liked to put a good hour or two in after their shifts were done for the day. Climbing gave them the challenge they needed to relieve any tension gained throughout the day and to build their climbing skills. Once engaged your mind focuses more on the task, allowing the mind to solve problems as it works to quickly plot a sequence of moves. Not only did it build strength, balance, flexibility, and endurance, all the ingredients for the athletic person, it was also just plain fun, and never boring. There were four routes one could take, offering months of climbing without repeating the same route. This made each route new and exciting.

As Laura watched she was also acting as a belayer who was employed to take up slack rope while the climber ascends. For her afternoon climb Jill chose the route of Top-Roping, which allowed her to be protected by a rope that runs through anchors placed above her intended route. Since Jill was a beginner this type of climbing allowed her to have a safe and exhilarating experience at heights usually reserved for more experienced climbers.

Fifteen minutes later Jill finished her route standing beside Laura, her dark blond, shoulder length hair tied in a pony tail bouncing with every move. Her face lit up with excitement over completing a successful climb as she smiled showing perfect white teeth. "That was the best, Laura. It's your turn again. Do you have time for one more?"

Laura looked at her watch. It was now four-ten and she had to be home by five-thirty. "Yes, I have time for one more." Walking over to the wall she reached up to start her climb when her pager beeped. "Oh great," she exclaimed, agitated while wondering what could her boss possibly want now? Quickly dialing his work number she listened to the rings, absently counting them.

"Yes Mr. Thatcher. What is the big emer—"

"Laura, you have to get over to the airport now! One of the airplanes due to land in about twenty minutes has a stowaway and animal control is on its way to assist."

"Okay, but this has happened before Jeff. Why couldn't one of the other vets take care of it?"

"Yes one could but I thought you would fit best since you have been researching the animal on a regular basis."

Laura's eyes grew round as the full impact of what he said sank in. "I'll be there in less than ten minutes."

"What's up," prompted Jill.

"I can't talk right now. I have to get to the airport. Call me later and give my love to Chad. He is growing so fast."

"Yes he is fourteen months now, as of yesterday. Talk to you later."

Laura picked up her gear and raced toward her car, forgetting to take off her harness. Running out of the parking lot she quickly located her Toyota. Placing her gear in the front seat beside her she got behind the wheel and was soon headed down the road. In seven minutes she entered the parking area for terminal one east. As she parked the car her phone beeped. Glancing at the display panel she saw a text from her boss. She quickly read it while exiting the car. Committing the plane's name and gate number to memory she entered the skybridge, to head toward gate two. Once there she took a shuttle over to the air control tower. Upon entering she was greeted by Mr. Bill Anderson, who was in charge.

"Good afternoon Mrs. Sinclair. We were expecting you. Follow me and I will take you to one of our monitors. The plane is due to land in five minutes."

Laura glanced at her watch and quickly noted the time while following Mr. Anderson to a monitor located at the south west side of the room. Beyond that was a huge window going from floor to ceiling, overlooking the runway that the plane was expected to land on, and which looked abandoned. Although, from the sidelines she could see those who were waiting, one group she recognized as animal control. She was brought back to the present at the sound of Mr. Anderson's voice.

"We have taken the liberty of running the feed through from the plane's monitor to our monitors here so that we can also see what is going on in the cargo hold. At first we could not believe what the pilots were trying to tell us until we saw it with our own eyes."

Laura's eyes also turned to the monitor in front of her. What she saw was totally amazing and beautiful. She was actually looking at a full grown, live Velociraptor. In all of her twenty-nine years she never thought it was possible. As she watched the Raptor she noted that something was terribly wrong. She was about to speak of it when Mr. Anderson shouted to all those in the room.

"Here she comes now!"

Laura looked in the direction of where he was pointing and she saw a huge white plane with the words ANA Cargo written on the side. The tail was painted all blue with the letters ANA written in white. As the plane approached the landing strip the landing gear moved into place. Moments later the ANA Cargo was coasting to a stop. Time seemed to stand still as the plane's engine grew quiet. Shortly after that the door near the front of the plane opened and the two pilots exited.

Laura looked again at the monitor. The Raptor was walking around but very slowly. At one point she moved over to a pile of tarp and lay down. "Mr. Anderson, how long has she been on the plane?"

"At least six hours. They left Costa Rica at ten-thirty this morning."

"What is the plane hauling?"

"Mostly perishables, like vegetables and fish."

"So the interior is kept cold at all times?"

"Yes of course."

There was part of the problem thought Laura.

"We have also noted," continued Mr. Anderson, "that one of the crates of fish broke open and the Raptor has been feasting on them."

That was the final answer Laura needed. The Raptor was slowly starving and freezing her-self to death. She knew what she had to do. Getting out her cell phone Laura dialed the number of the animal control team, who had been waiting for her instructions. Mr. Lance Turner answered so Laura filled him in on what she wanted done. Soon Laura's voice showed agitation.

"What do you mean you refuse?"

"I am sorry Mrs. Sinclair. I am not going near that creature while it is awake."

"Fine then, you just prepare things for me as I ask and I will do it. Meet me at the plane in twenty minutes, and hurry or we will lose her." Laura hung up the phone, seething. "Mr. Anderson. Could I persuade you to shuttle me out to the plane?"

Minutes later Laura found herself standing at the bottom of the steps leading to the flight deck. When Lance finally appeared she gave him a steely look and took the package he proffered. Turning she walked up the stairs and into the plane. Mr. Anderson had instructed her on how to open the door and close it fast if she needed to. As she approached the entrance the enormity of what she was about to do hit her. Shaking her head she brushed the feelings aside. This had to be done. She just hoped she would still be around later so Bradley could kill her for being so reckless.

Positioning the package in front of her she opened it to reveal a huge piece of meat. Inside, it contained a tranquilizer measured to the animals size and estimated weight. When finished she opened the door and stepped inside.

* * * * *

Day 2 mid afternoon

The mother raptor slept in her nest. She felt so cold, the muscles in her body stiffening up. Not even the landing of the plane had an effect on her. She lay there for awhile until a scent touched her nostrils that she recognized, which was also mixed with that of a two-legger. All senses on the alert she stood up and moved out of the nest on shaky legs. Moving around a crate she came face-to-face with the two-legger. Releasing a screech she lowered her head to charge but then suddenly pulled back. There was something very different concerning this two-legger. The mother raptor watched her as she bent down to release an object that fell between them. Her nose immediately detected the scent of fresh meat. Moving toward it the mother raptor relished the scent. The meat quickly disappeared in two quick bites. Bringing her head up the mother raptor looked again at the two-legger. Now that she was closer by at least eight feet two things quickly became evident, the two-legger was female and she wore the harness. This two-legger was a climber, the one she was looking for. Immediately she started making soft clicking noises while walking up to the two-legger. She sniffed the harness, pulling on it with her teeth. She then moved to nudge the two-legger with her nose, rubbing as if scent marking, the force of it almost knocking Laura off her feet. Laura stood her ground, not moving but taking careful mental notes of the raptors actions. Soon the mother raptor began to stumble in her movements. In less than five minutes she was asleep.

* * * * *

As soon as the Raptor collapsed Laura moved into action, part of which involved going to the outside entrance to tell Lance and his team it was safe to come up. When Lance entered he swore under his breath as he approached the Raptor.

"Are you sure she is knocked out?"

Laura gave him an irritated look. "The tranquilizer immobilizes the muscles. She is aware of her surroundings but she just can't move. It is imperative that we get her to the zoo's clinic because she should not remain in this state for long. So let us not quibble over little things and do our jobs. Now let's get going." Lance nodded in agreement.

Once the Raptor was placed in the back of a van designed to specifically transport wild animals they left for the zoo. For this trip Laura rode in the back with the Raptor. Her reasons were simple. Because the animal's muscles were weakened she could succumb to stress very quickly. Laura wanted to reduce those chances so she sat beside the Raptor's head, allowing the Raptor to see her while Laura rubbed the animal on the nose and face. Being this close to such a predator was awe-inspiring. This presented another factor as to why she road in the back. For some reason the Raptor let her live and she was determined to find out why.

After a short thirteen minute ride the vehicle pulled into the San Diego Zoo to park in front of the zoo's clinic. From there Laura again took charge, making sure the utmost care was given while moving the Raptor. Not only was there the chance of stress but also pain. A careless bump against a wall or collision with a door could be hazardess. Once the Raptor was placed inside their enclosed tiger cage, which was used to hold tigers or other big cats before and after surgery and to monitor their condition, Laura went to work. Taking quick measurements and recording the result she mentally checked for any serious wounds. Finding none she gave the Raptor a shot of antibiotics. Once done she injected the final shot that would give muscle control back to the Raptor then quickly left the cage, locking the door behind her. In less than a minute the Raptor was shakily climbing to her feet. Finding a huge pile of raw meat at one end of the cage, left earlier by one of the veterinarian aids, she feasted. Laura watched her, fascinated.

Just to make sure the Raptor was adapting well Laura stayed for another hour. Only then did she leave to go home. Once there she received a serious lecture from Bradley, who had just arrived home from his business trip, on the risks and lives involved for being so reckless. The airport had taken the liberty of using the video take of her entire encounter with the Raptor and displayed it on the evening news, which did not help her cause. Part of her escape of his tongue lashing was feigning exhaustion, which wasn't far from the truth. She was exhausted. After a quick shower she crawled under the covers beside a still unhappy husband.

Day 3

The next morning found Laura walking through the double doors of the zoo's clinic. The usual commotion greeted her as she noted aids and other veterinarians moving about in their care for the zoo's animals. The only two differences was the female Raptor, who was quietly observing the goings on in the room while resting in the nest the aids had constructed before her arrival; and her boss, who was quite busy on the opposite side of the room supervising the installation of a television. Laura shook her head, puzzled at his actions but not overly anxious to find the answers. Instead she approached an aid for a report of the night's activities, especially on the Raptor. The report lasted for a good twenty minutes revealing pretty much the same as other nights, except for the Raptor. It seems she spent a lot of her time working on the nest, as though preparing it for young ones. Laura took note of this and set about starting her morning duties.

The mother raptor watched her every move. During the night she had briefly explored the outside enclosed yard, taking note of the different smells and surroundings. Once back inside she settled in the nest to watch other two-leggers work with strange looking creatures. Her attention changed when Laura entered the room.

As Laura worked she tried her best to ignore her boss as he continued his task of supervising the TV's installation. It wasn't to last long before he approached her. She could tell he was near without even looking because of the hideous smelling cologne he always wore.

"Laura, there is something I would like to show you."

Knowing that she could not deny his presence any longer she turned to face him. She quickly noted his appearance. Being only a few inches taller than her five feet, eight inches Thatcher never ceased to amaze her as to how good looking he was. Today he was dressed in a pressed light blue shirt, brown tie, and dark brown dress pants. Laura could see that he had not gotten a chance to shave this morning as evidence of the short stubble covering a square jaw. His nose was straight and narrow, but his eyes were the most prominent. They were such a light blue that they looked like glass. Right now his pupils were so small, resembling a narrow, up and down oval, giving the appearance of a reptile; a glass-eyed reptile. His eyebrows were thick, dark brown to match his hair, which was cut short. Although these features may be appealing they did not hide what he was like on the inside. Selfish, conceited, sneaky, and conniving were just a few choice ones she could think of. He always attempted to be in control while wanting and needing things to go his way. Laura braced herself for what was to come.

"All right, if it does not take too long. I have quite a bit of work to do."

"It won't take long. Come over here." With that he touched her arm as though to guide her. No sooner had he done that did the Raptor screech loudly, charging toward him but stopping when she reached the steel bars of the cage. Everyone in the room jumped while cries of excitement and alarm issued from the animals. After the initial shock Laura was impressed.

"I don't think I would do that again Thatcher." Laura smiled inside as she saw him fidget.

"Well, I just wanted to show you how to operate the TV."

"I know how to operate one."

Good, just make sure you have it on at three p.m. today. They are broadcasting a special event on your dinosaur. I feel that this animal will bring a lot of business to the zoo. People are going to come from all over to see her,"

"Thatcher, you are not planning on keeping her."

"I am in the process of negotiating with the Costa Rican government to allow us to do just that."

"No, you are supposed to contact them and make arrangements to send her back."

"Things change. Just make sure you watch the show." With that he turned and left the room.

Laura stared daggers at his back. She was definitely adding greed to that descriptive list of hers. For the rest of the morning Laura spent feeding the tiger cubs and working with one of the primates. This primate was a chimpanzee named Charlie. He had once belonged to a circus but had been so abused that animal rescue had to step in. They, of course, brought him to the zoo to live. That was two years ago and now Charlie was recovering from a nasty cold. Whenever Laura had the opportunity to examine Charlie she made it a point to make it fun for him because he was prone to bouts of depression. For this she used some of his favorite games, two of which were called 'Yes and No' and 'Counting.' Today they would focus on Counting in the hope of getting him to use his ability to use sign language. To begin the game Laura arranged cards with pictures on them of flowers, lady bugs, and butterflies. Then it was Charlie's job to identify them by counting them when prompted. After the game was over

Charlie had other ideas by insisting on playing the Yes and No game. Laura had no choice but to give in.

Five minutes into the game it was Charlie's turn to ask a question. Laura's task was to answer the question correctly by only saying yes, or no. Charlie made the sign for baby. Laura smiled and, putting her left hand on her abdomen signed, "Yes." Charlie shook his head fast in the negative causing Laura to frown. Charlie signed, 'get baby.' Laura answered yes. Charlie agreed then signed, 'sad baby.' Laura answered no. With that Charlie turned animated as he shook his head fast and signed, 'wrong, wrong' over and over. Laura had had enough and signed for Charlie to stop and the game was finished for the day. Handing Charlie over to one of the aids she walked over to look at the Raptor. It was at that moment that her husband entered. Seeing she faced away from him he thought to surprise her. The mother raptor saw him approaching and as he reached out to touch Laura she released an alarm call and left the nest, making a mock, but still meaningful charge. Laura turned and smiled when she saw Bradley.

"Hi Bradley."

"Hi, so what's up with her?" he asked, pointing toward the Raptor.

"I am not quite sure but she is very protective of me. She did this earlier too. She throws a fit if someone tries to touch me."

"Well I might give her a bit of a challenge because to touch you is my distinct privilege."

Laura smiled, "I doubt she will win that fight." It was then that Laura remembered something. "My dear, I need you to help me out with something, just a small experiment. I want you to stand completely still, and don't move until I tell you to. It is important." Bradley looked puzzled but complied. Laura approached him. Using the left side of her face, shoulder, and arm she brushed against his left shoulder and arm. When finished the lower part of her back and hip touched his hand. Turning she walked behind him to his right side and did the same. When she was completely finished she stood directly in front of him.

"Okay now attempt to touch me Bradley."

Her husband reached up to touch her arm. The Raptor was silent, remaining in her nest.

"It worked!" exclaimed Laura.

"Okay, so what just happened?"

"I think you have just been welcomed into the family."

"That's nice. Well this family member is hungry. Would my beautiful wife care to join me for lunch?"

"She would love to."

Twenty minutes later they were both sitting at the Olive Garden restaurant waiting for their food orders to arrive. In the mean time they munched on salad and breadsticks. Bradley was the first to speak.

"So what were you doing when I first walked in?"

"Well I was trying to figure out what would make the Raptor come here, over thousands of miles, when it is the spring of the year and she should be with her babies. It is quite obvious that she is nesting. Something is very wrong. It does not make sense. I also get the feeling that she is trying to communicate. I just have to figure out her language."

"What do you mean by language?"

"People are the only species with the ability to form words from their thoughts and place them into a voice pattern. Animals communicate by using two distinct methods, sound and their bodies. Think of the experiment I did earlier as an example. The Raptor did that same thing to me on the plane. It was as if she were saying, 'you are okay.' The one major thing that puzzles me is why she grabbed the climbing harness."

Conversation ceased for a moment as the waitress appeared with their food. She quickly set their plates on the table in front of them and left. For a bit no one spoke as they started to eat. Bradley soon broke the silence.

"I have confidence in you Laura. You will figure it out."

Laura released a sigh. "I hope so. I just hope I don't find out before it is too late."

The rest of the meal was eaten in silence as they soon finished, paid for the meal, and drove back to the zoo. By the time Laura walked through the door after kissing her husband goodbye it was one thirty. There was plenty of time to get some more work done before the three o'clock broadcast. As she started Laura noted that the Raptor had been outside but returned to the nest when she walked into the room. If she did not know better she would think the Raptor was trying to follow her.

As the two o'clock hour approached Laura heard a very familiar voice shout a greeting her way. She looked up to see her friend Jill walking toward her carrying her fourteen month old son, Chad. When halfway there Jill set Chad down and he walked toward Laura, who had bent down on one knee to greet the child. Scooping him up in her arms Laura hugged him.

"Hey, how is the little man today?" she asked, looking at Chad. He looked at her with wide eyes while pointing at her face. Laura smiled, and then turned to look at Jill.

"He seems to be in the point-at-everything stage," said Jill. She reached over to take Chad. "I thought I would stop by to see if you wanted to do some climbing this weekend. My mom said that she would watch Chad while we go." At that moment Chad started to squirm so Laura set him down.

"I don't think I have anything planned. Sure, why not. What time did you want to leave?"

"I have an appointment Saturday morning. How about meeting for dinner at a restaurant that serves good salads and we can leave after that."

"That sounds good Jill. I will make sure to note it in my planner."

They both jumped when something crashed behind them to the floor, followed quickly by a scream. Then the whole room grew silent. They both turned and Laura heard Jill scream beside her and Laura's eyes grew round in shocked surprise as she looked at the Raptor, now standing up, looking at them; from her mouth hung Chad, dangling by his shirt collar. The child was laughing, enjoying the swinging motion and totally oblivious to the danger he was in. Everyone watched as the mother raptor turned, walked up to her nest and gently placed the child inside. She then stepped carefully in the nest and around Chad. Lying down next to him she started to make soft clicking noises, which attracted Laura's attention immediately. As she listened Laura understood what was happening.

"He is going to be okay, Jill."

"What do you mean? She is going to eat my baby!"

"No, she is not. If that was the case Chad would be gone already. I have seen this type of behavior before. In Pichit, Thailand a cat found a baby mouse in a closet and treated it as a kitten. In Paarl, South Africa a mother cat nursed three baby squirrels that fell out of their nest during a storm. We have also had similar experiences here at the zoo. The Raptor has adopted Chad as one of her own."

"I don't care. I want my little boy back!"

Hearing his mother's voice Chad decided to be with her and began to climb out of the nest. The mother raptor raised her head to watch. Soft clicking noises sounded again. Moving across the cage floor and up to the bars Chad walked. Seeing his mom on the other side he slipped through the bars and walked over to her. Jill snatched him up as soon as he was within reach, holding him close. Everyone in the room began to relax.

Jill and Laura examined Chad for any kind of injuries, but none were found. After a brief calming down period Jill took Chad home. By the time three o'clock rolled around the clinic was back to its normal routine. The TV on the south wall suddenly came on automatically, blasting the room with sound. It was obvious Thatcher had installed a timer.

Laura watched the show for a good twenty minutes when she was joined again by her husband. He had finished working for the day and wanted to watch the broadcast with her. While they did she related what had happened over the past hour. At first Bradley was shocked but then he started to see a pattern when he applied what his wife said over dinner earlier, and now with Chad. After the show he would tell her his theory.

As the show progressed they were able to view the video of the time on the airplane when the Raptor was alone and during the encounter with Laura. Then the narrator talked some about the island and the species, showing what others thought the Raptor's lifestyle was like. When a nest containing eggs hatching was shown the mother raptor started making the soft clicking noises. Laura turned her head to look at the Raptor, noting that she was also watching. Laura looked at her husband and he nodded. Five minutes later the show ended. Laura turned away from the set to talk to Bradley when the Raptor started the soft clicking noises again. Laura stopped, looked at the Raptor, then the TV. A commercial was playing, advertising the Solid Rock Climbing Gym. The Raptor continued the clicking until the commercial was gone.

"I don't know about you Laura but I can see a connection here. It is obvious from what you have told me and what I have seen here that the main focus is the mountain climbing gear and the babies. She is trying to connect them."

As Laura listened to her husband Charlie's words during the yes/no game suddenly ran through her head, get baby, sad baby over and over. "Also animals can sense fear or tension from other animals. My god Bradley, you don't think she came all this way to ask for our help, do you?"

Bradley shook his head in disbelief. "I think so. It is hard to believe, but ya. Stranger things have happened."

"Good news, good news," spoke a voice from behind them. "I just got off the phone with the Costa Rican government and they said, as long as there are no problems, we can keep the Raptor."

Laura turned slightly to see Thatcher walk up to their small group.

"Just think of it Laura, you will be able to expand your research, which you have been so eager to pursue."

"In their natural habitat, not caged like this," replied Laura, nodding her head in the direction of the Raptor. "Also the Raptor is NOT staying. She is going home, tonight!"

"I'm sorry Laura, but you don't have a say in this. You are not the boss here."

Suddenly Laura had had enough of her boss. Even the mere sight of him sickened her. "Well then you will just have to fire me, or maybe I should just quit. Save you the trouble. I am sick and tired of you throwing your weight around. I think it is high time you grow up and think of others instead of only yourself."

All at once the whole room erupted in applause.

"I guess I am not the only one who will be quitting," stated Laura.

"Well said," stated Bradley.

Thatcher knew he wasn't going to win this fight since it was obvious he was out numbered so he tried a different tactic. "Fine then, have it your way. I think you are making a big mistake. You saw the broadcast; people are going to flock here, to this zoo, in the thousands. This can help the zoo and its employees." Those in the room just stared at him with steely expressions. The pleading for a good cause ploy definitely failed. "Okay, since you are so determined to take her out of here then I feel that I should go along as well." He then turned and left the room, not giving Laura a chance to respond. Laura rolled her eyes and made an exasperated sound. After the door closed behind Thatcher, Laura turned to her husband.

"May we use your company jet?"

"Of course my beautiful spitfire, since I happen to own the company you may use the plane anytime; but you know I plan on coming too." Laura hugged him close. She loved him dearly and would never be whole or complete unless he was in her life.

The next few hours were spent getting things ready to go. Bradley left to get the plane ready while Laura worked with the Raptor. Others also volunteered to help. A shiny steel barred cage was found that was used to move big cats, but for this time a Raptor would have access. Since using the van to move the animal was easier, the cage was moved to the plane empty.

When Bradley called to say the plane was ready for take-off that was Laura's cue to bring the Raptor. Once again she placed a type of tranquilizer in a chunk of meat and gave it to the Raptor. A few minutes later several aids and ground attendants carried the two hundred pound, five point nine foot long Raptor to the van and gently placed her inside. After making sure she was comfortable Laura climbed inside and sat near her head. Talking soothingly to her Laura rubbed her nose and face as the mother raptor watched her. Once secure the van moved out of the zoo parking lot.

A few minutes later the van pulled up beside the plane. As Laura exited the van she looked at the sleek, smooth lines of the aircraft. A Boeing Business Jet specifically designed to allow the leader of a large corporation or a free-wheeling entrepreneur to conduct their business in comfort and style. Up to twenty passengers could take advantage of its comfort and versatility but in this instance only three people and one Raptor would be its passengers.

Entering the plane Laura looked to see what arrangements had been done. It was obvious the plane would have to be remodeled somewhat. Laura noted that the area near the back of the plane had been rearranged. Reclining chairs and a couch were placed against the walls, a huge blanket or rug was placed over the floor and the cage placed on top. Satisfied Laura went back outside to supervise the transfer. With the help from the volunteers, who had followed in another vehicle, they were able to place the mother raptor in the cage. Once inside Laura reached through the bars to inject the shot that would wake the Raptor up. For the next few minutes Laura kept a close eye on her to make sure all was good. Once she was satisfied Laura told her husband it was okay to leave. Bradley informed the pilot and after a quick arrival from Thatcher the doors closed. From there the engines started; allowing the plane to coast up to a certain speed down the runway, then lift into the air, heading for Costa Rica.

During the five hour trip Laura spent most of the time sitting near the Raptor in one of the reclining chairs. Bradley sat in a chair nearby while Thatcher reclined on one of the couches. The mother raptor was able to rest in a small nest placed in the back of the square cage. There were moments when they got up to stretch their legs. During this time Laura would feed the Raptor choice cuts of beef in huge chunks. Since they left San Diego at ten p.m. Laura expected to land at Palmar Sur around three a.m., weather permitting. That settled, along with the Raptor satisfactorily full she decided it was time for some shut eye. Grabbing a blanket and pillow she settled back into the recliner and was soon asleep, followed soon by Bradley and Thatcher.

Two hours before landing Laura suddenly woke up. She wasn't quite sure why but she felt uneasy. Shaking the sleepy, groggy feeling away she brought her eyes into focus. Looking around she saw that Thatcher was no longer in his seat, most likely in the bathroom, and Bradley was asleep across from her. What she saw beside her husband made her sit bolt upright. The mother raptor saw her and acknowledged Laura's presence by clicking softly. She then turned back to investigating Bradley. Laura watched, not daring to move while her mind raced for a solution. Her thoughts centered suddenly on communication and sound. It was worth a try so she mimicked the clicking noise the Raptor had just done. It wasn't the greatest, but was close enough because the Raptor turned to look at her and Laura automatically nodded her head to say yes. It was at that moment that the restroom door across the cabin opened and Thatcher stepped out, stopping when he saw the Raptor. The Raptor turned at the intrusion, screeched and charged. Knowing there was nothing holding her back this time Laura reacted on instinct and shouted, "NO!" The Raptor stopped five feet from reaching Thatcher, tail whipping from side to side she lowered her head and hissed at him, flexing her two front sickle-like talons, while tapping the distinctive one on the second toe of her foot.

"Thatcher, I don't know how long I can hold her back. I would advise you to move carefully back into the restroom."

Thatcher did not hesitate and moved back into the restroom, locking the door behind him. Once Thatcher was out of sight the Raptor calmed down. She turned around, walked up to Laura, nudged her to acknowledge that all was well, and then returned to her nest to sleep. Laura took that opportunity to close the cage door and double lock it. Once the Raptor was secure again she told Thatcher it was okay to come out. She then settled back in her chair.

"Honey, could you keep that Raptor quiet please," mumbled Bradley.

Laura looked at her husband as he slept, while fighting the urge to laugh, uncontrollably. She did chuckle a bit when she saw Thatcher roll his eyes then fall onto the couch. That was impressive, but what was even more impressive was the response from the Raptor to the words yes and no. Laura had no idea that the animal had been that observant while at the clinic. Laura wondered what other things the Raptor had learned.

By three a.m. the plane had landed in Palmar Sur. Bradley left to see if the boat they had made arrangements for was ready, although this was after an extended explanation of why the couch had slash marks all over, and a good half hour for her husband to recover. Thatcher also left for reasons he only knew of and Laura could care less about.

Day 4

By eight a.m. the boat was loaded with supplies, equipment, and one curious Raptor. They were able to find a boat that would give them the speed they needed, allow them to carry the cage with the Raptor, and give them living quarters for the time they were at the island. The Costa Rican government even gave them the go ahead since it was explained that the zoo had 'changed its mind' and decided to return the Raptor. With fair winds and a good weather report the boat sailed through the waters, making good time. By one thirty the vessel was approaching Ancient Rock. Laura knew it was time and turned to Thatcher, who was watching the island.

"Thatcher, you need to go down below so that the Raptor does not see you."

For a moment he looked confused, but only for a moment then he disappeared below. Laura walked over to the cage with Bradley close behind and opened the door. The Raptor burst out and ran over to the side of the boat. She turned to look at Laura who nodded her head. Confirmation given the Raptor searched for just the right boulder and leapt. Laura was impressed with the distance the Raptor could achieve. Once her footing was set the rest was easy as she followed parallel with the boat, which entered a small gulf near Ancient Rock. Once the boat was secure Laura prepared to go ashore. The captain, a portly little man helped get the row boat ready by placing Laura's gear inside then lowering it into the water. During that time Laura talked with her husband reassuring him that all would be well and that she had to do this by herself. He finally, but reluctantly agreed when she insisted that she would keep her two way radio close by her and call him if needed.

Bradley watched Laura as she rowed to shore. His heart was in that boat, his whole life. He could not bear it if anything happened to her or their baby, but she was right and he knew it. She was the animal expert and he would most likely get in the way.

Once the row boat touched ground Laura got out and pulled the boat away from the lapping waves. Securing her gear she walked onto dry ground. The mother raptor greeted her, and then arching her neck she called her pack. Soon the beach was full of raptors. A heated discussion between the mother raptor ensued as she explained Laura's presence, to be followed by a tender greeting from the alpha male. Once done they moved into the forest with Laura following the mother raptor. In a short while Laura entered a small clearing, surrounded by tall trees and ferns. Enclosed within were three nests and as Laura counted the hatchlings she noted that each nest contained twelve except one, which had eleven.

Setting her equipment down she put her climbing harness on and grabbed the necessary things she would need, anchors, rappel device, cams, ropes, etc. Once she was ready she nodded affirmative to the mother raptor and she took off leading the way. Traveling half a mile through trees and ferns they emerged into a clearing. Other raptors had gone ahead to make sure it was safe. Laura could see the cliff on the opposite side. Knowing her goal she still waited for the Raptor's guidance. She was in the raptors world now and the rules were quite different. Once it was deemed safe Laura moved forward. She knew her time was limited because she was out in the open so when she reached the cliff's edge she set to work.

Her job was to make a controlled slide down a fixed rope, a double-rope rappel that would allow her to get down faster. Setting her bolt in place she secured the rope. She then tied another climbing rope using a double figure-8 fisherman's knot. Finding the end of each rope she placed tie stopper knots so she would not rappel off the end. Finally she settled on an auto block knot as a safety back-up. To control the descent and to help utilize the friction of the rope Laura used a rappel device. Clearing up a few loose ends and double checking her knots she was ready to go. She was suddenly startled from her work when she heard the alarmed alert from one of the raptors. Immediately a wall was formed around her, facing the threat. Laura looked in that direction and her jaw dropped open. Charging toward them was a bull T-Rex.

* * * * *

The air was quiet around the nesting site. The hatchlings were resting while waiting for the adults to return. While not planning on being gone long the adults felt that having more eyes to spot danger and deal with it the faster they would be able to return. The one thing they did not figure on was another type of predator that would dare to enter the nesting site. This predator entered boldly, walking up to a nest. Thatcher looked down at the sleeping babies. Pick of the litter he thought. He was beside himself when he decided to grab one of the babies for his own, which was why he insisted on coming along. What a neat idea and he set about putting his plan in motion. When Bradley wasn't watching Thatcher snitched another row boat. Once ashore he set about tracking Laura, which wasn't difficult. That was one thing he was good at, tracking his prey. Now he reached into his pocket and extracted a small piece of cloth and a clear bottle of chloroform. He could not afford having the little one make a sound. In a few minutes he had one safely tucked inside a shoulder bag. He then used a long fern to wipe his scent away and race to meet the helicopter he had arranged to meet at a specified clearing.

* * * * *

Laura knew the raptors would not stand a chance against a frontal attack so she shouted, "No." The mother raptor looked at her and Laura shook her head, repeating the word no and motioning for them to leave. She then picked up her rope and repelled over the edge. The mother raptor gave the command and the pack scattered, giving the T-Rex air to snap at. From that the raptors easily maneuvered the T-Rex away from the cliff by offering themselves as lures to lead him away. For Laura she had to deal with a little falling rock and dirt but all was good. She made it safely to a ledge. Walking along it she discovered a dead dinosaur and a nest. There wasn't much left but its feet, hands, and legs. Looking in the nest she found what she was looking for, a baby Raptor. He looked up at her with wondering eyes and she smiled. Giving him a quick examination she found that he was doing well, with only a trace of dehydration and lack of motherly comfort. It was obvious the little one had fed on the dead dinosaur and, as she looked in the nest, the adults had regurgitated food over the cliff's edge. Picking the hatchling up she placed it in a pet carrier bag strapped to her chest. Making sure he was secure she checked her knots, especially the one tied onto her harness and began her climb back up. When she came close to cresting the side of the cliff she cautiously approached the top, listening for any strange sounds. Satisfied she finished her climb and found the area totally abandoned. Not waiting for an explanation she quickly collected her gear and made for the woods. Halfway there she stopped, sensing something was wrong. Looking to her right she saw the T-Rex as he stepped out of the forest and into the clearing. Even though Laura was standing still the animal did have a keen sense of smell and if the wind was wrong—the T-Rex looked at her. The wind was wrong and Laura moved to run just as a rush of wind moved around and past her as the raptors rushed in to deflect the T-Rex as it charged toward Laura. While they did that the mother raptor went up to Laura and led her into the forest and safety. A few different turns and swerves brought Laura back to the nesting site. In a short while the rest of the pack arrived.

Laura approached one of the nests and brought the pet carrier forward, setting it on the edge of a nest. Unzipping the carrier she reached inside and extracted the baby. She held it up so they all could see, then she lowered it to the nest and watched him scamper in with the others. One of the raptors sniffed at it. Soft clicking noises ensued.

Laura sat on the edge of the nest watching the babies play. It was at that moment the characteristically sweet odor of chloroform reached her. Looking down at her feet she saw a small piece of cloth. Picking it up Laura said, "Thatcher!" She abruptly turned, catching the attention of the mother raptor. Laura started counting the babies.

One was missing from the second nest. Laura mouthed the word no and shook her head. This alerted the mother raptor and she understood. Another baby was missing. It was then that Laura heard the distant sound of a helicopter. Signaling to the mother raptor Laura took off for the clearing at a dead run. She had to hurry or Thatcher would get away.

* * * * *

Thatcher watched the helicopter lower the ladder. Shifting the small shoulder bag to his left side he reached for the closest wrung on the ladder and began to climb. Halfway up he felt a tug on his leg. Puzzled he looked down and gasped in horror. His left leg was gone. Then he saw the jaws, the jagged sharp teeth, and eyes of the T-Rex. Thatcher screamed.

Just as Thatcher screamed Laura made it to the edge of the forest in time to see the T-Rex grab Thatcher from the ladder and swallow him in two gulps. She closed her eyes and looked away.

After the T-Rex roared its anger at the escaping helicopter did Laura turn to look? Frustrated the T-Rex sauntered back into the forest to join with his family, and then all was quiet. Looking at the spot where Thatcher had been Laura noted something lying in the grass. She pointed to it and, shaking her head said, "Yes." The mother raptor left the forest's edge and walked up to the object, sniffed at it, then gingerly picked it up and carried it to Laura. A few minutes later they were back at the nesting site. Laura took the bag and set it gently on the side of a nest. Opening the bag she carefully extracted the hatchling then placed her on top of the bag to examine her. No bones were broken and the hatchling was breathing all right. Laura then turned to her supplies and retrieved her medical bag. She started searching through its contents, and searched. In the very bottom of the bag she found it, ever so glad she did not get anxious about inconsequential things lingering in the bottom of her bag and throw them out. Opening the small bottle of smelling salts she placed it in a small wave back and forth under the hatchling's nose. Soon the little one jerked awake, lifting herself to her feet. Looking at Laura she yawned. Laura smiled and picked up the hatchling and placed her in the second nest. The mother raptor walked over to Laura and nudged her. Laura reached over and rubbed her nose.

"Your welcome, mother raptor," said Laura.

After collecting her gear, talking briefly to Bradley, and taking some pictures she started to leave. She did not get far when the mother raptor blocked her path. Puzzled Laura looked at her. Several sharp clicking noises ensued. Two other raptors came forward, one standing on each side of Laura. She then understood as the mother raptor moved out of her way and Laura left with her escort.

A few minutes later Laura was on board the boat being warmly greeted by her husband. Since it was getting dark they decided to spend the night. Come morning Laura awoke to a short, continuous, trumpeting bark. Quickly dressing Laura went on deck and saw the mother raptor calling her.

"What's wrong?" asked Bradley as he walked up behind her.

"For some reason she wants me to come back. Well I might as well go see what she wants."

Grabbing her medicine bag, the two-way radio, and a camcorder she met with the Raptor. The mother raptor then proceeded to escort her to a small hill over looking a valley and down in that valley Laura got to witness, for the first time a hunt in progress. She watched as they selected their prey from a herd, separating it from the rest, and then going in for the kill. She made special note of how they used their tails as a counter balance allowing the Raptor to make very quick turns.

After the hunt Laura was escorted back to the nesting site where she spent time with the hatchlings, watching how they were fed and cared for. Laura thought it was amazing when she realized that the mother raptor was showing and sharing her world with Laura.

The following weeks were pretty much the same and Laura was able to glean a lot of information. She was even able to view the bull T-Rex and his mate, plus the bonus of seeing their two beautiful twin calves. Time had gone by so fast when Laura had realized a whole month had passed. She knew that she would need to leave because soon her own pregnancy would be evident.

One day, early she approached the mother raptor as she sat near the nests. Reaching down she picked up one of the babies running around by her feet. She rubbed its tummy and it clicked softly, enjoying the massage while the mother raptor watched. Laura placed the baby back down and clicking softly nodded yes. Straightening back up Laura touched her hand to her stomach, which at six months was showing a rounded abdomen, and clicked softly then nodded yes. The mother raptor nudged Laura's stomach and clicked softly. She understood.

Once again Laura's escorts were chosen. She noted during the choice and during the hours she was on the island that there was one Raptor that always seemed to be on the outside of the group, somewhat like a rebel. Laura would have liked to try asking the mother raptor but she knew that it was time to leave and it was important to leave while it was light out so the boat would make it through the gulf and past the rocks safely. Before she left she said goodbye to the mother raptor in the familiar way but adding a hug at the end. Then Laura and her two escorts left. No one noticed that another soon left the pack.

A short while later Laura and her escorts were passing through a small clearing and Laura grew uneasy. Something did not feel right and she suddenly wished she was on the boat. In that moment of thought one of her escorts lay dead beside her, its side sliced open. Laura jumped and the other escort sounded an alarm call just as the rebel jumped onto its back from behind. Laura saw the sickle-like claw on the rear foot as it cut into the side of the second escort, and the jaws close over the back of its neck, snapping and slicing in one instant, then the escort was dead.

Back at the nests the sound of that alarm call reached the ears of the mother raptor. She immediately raced off in its direction, most of her pack in tow.

Moving off the second escort the rebel now faced Laura. Whipping its tail from side to side the rebel lowered its head hissing, while taking a couple of steps toward Laura. Flexing his two front sickle-like talons the rebel prepared to jump. Stopping in mid crouch he suddenly screeched loudly at Laura. Laura noted a sudden change as well. She was no longer alone. Standing on her left side was the mother raptor and a young adult. On her right were the alpha male and another older Raptor. The rebel started to back up but stopped as the rest of the pack appeared, forming a circle around him. The alpha male and the mother raptor moved forward, approaching the rebel. Laura could tell this was not going to be good.

"Mother raptor, please don't," said Laura as she shook her head.

The mother raptor turned toward Laura and hissed, screeching loudly. Laura understood and lowered her head in submission. She was now attending court and the two lead Raptor's judgments were final. For some reason the rebel had reached its final straw. There was no turning back.

Laura watched as both alphas walked up to the rebel, each using combinations of clicking, screeching, hissing, and other sounds Laura had not heard before. Suddenly the alpha male turned, delivering a blow to the side of the rebel, leaving a huge bleeding welt. The rebel screeched, moving toward the alpha female, who in turn delivered a welt to its other side. This caused the rebel to move back. Once done the two alphas moved to stand beside Laura and the pack moved in. Soon there was nothing left of the rebel but a bloody mass of flesh.

After all was done the pack disappeared and the two alphas finished escorting Laura to the beach. Once there a number of rubbing sessions ensued to say goodbye and to give the assurance that all was well once again. Laura would miss them very much; after all she was a member of the pack, their family.

Later, as Laura stood on the deck of the boat she watched the beach recede away and soon the island itself. She knew she would never forget them. Turning into her husband's arms he held her close as she cried.

* * * * *

Six months later the mother raptor watched the two-legger on the fishing boat dump some more waste into the ocean. She waited as some floated toward the beach. When all was safe she left her hiding place and retrieved one of them. Placing it in the grass she looked at the image. Soft clicking noises ensued as she saw Laura and Bradley standing close together and in Laura's arms she held their infant son. If the Raptor could have read it would have told her of the praise for the in depth research conducted by Laura concerning the raptors and her promotion as the new zoo's manager. Arching her head the mother raptor sent a call out. Soon she was joined by another young Raptor, which had spent his first few days of life on the side of a cliff. The mother raptor drew attention to the image and the young one acknowledged it. He also remembered the two-legger. Once they were done they both moved off into the forest, leaving the magazine behind.

PART TWO

A MOTHER'S LOVE FOR THAT OF A MATE

The sun shown brightly, sending its warmth to those who moved on the earth's surface. A soft breeze moved through the trees, lightly touching Laura as she sat on the porch watching her son play. She was glad there was a child safety gate blocking the entrance to the porch as her son toppled over, landing with a soft thud against the barrier. Going from crawling to standing at nine months was a wonderful transition to observe. Just before he fell he had been walking while holding onto the bars of the safety gate. When he reached the end he decided to let go offering him the opportunity to stand alone for a few seconds before his wobbly legs gave out. As Laura watched her son, whom she named Jayden push him-self to a sitting position she noted his nose wrinkle with displeasure. She could sense he was getting tired. Even so he was not going to give up. Reaching out with his small hands Jayden took hold of the bars and pulled him-self up to a standing position, little legs jerking with the effort. Arriving at the end of the gate he moved to stand alone again. Laura reached her arms out to him. Spying them

Jayden laughed gleefully, his eyes sparkling with life. Taking one step he promptly lost his balance, landing on his bottom. That was the final straw as Laura saw tears forming. Smiling Laura walked over to him and picked him up.

"You are such a brave little boy and so independent."

Walking into the house Laura carried Jayden upstairs and placed him in his crib. In a few short minutes he was asleep. For a moment she stood looking at his sleeping features and she smiled, thinking of the evident and soon to be evident features Jayden carried from his father. Instead of a round jaw both have square with dark complexions. If Jayden's eyes were open they would be the reflection of her own.

"Mistress Laura?"

Laura looked up to see Rosa standing in the doorway. She smiled, placing her finger over her mouth to signify silence. Rosa nodded and stepped back into the hall. Laura followed her after making sure the infant monitor was working properly. Meeting by the stairway Laura asked, "What is it Rosa?"

"There is a man downstairs. He says he wishes to speak with you."

"Really, I wonder what he wants. Thank you Rosa."

Rosa nodded and left to finish her duties. Laura walked down the steps and into the foyer. The man stood near the door and when Laura saw him her first impression was not good. Standing a good five feet, ten inches he gave the instant image of one who commanded an aura of authority. His eyes were hard but shifty. He attempted to smile a greeting, which enhanced his high cheekbones and protruding jaw. As she shook his hand she was met with a sweaty, clammy palm. She knew she could not trust this man but she was also curious as to what he wanted. Maybe he was just a fan of her work?

"Good afternoon Mrs. Sinclair. It is so nice to finally meet you. My name is Vince Davis and I would like to talk to you, if you have a few minutes?"

"Of course, please follow me."

Leading him into the living room she offered him a seat on a soft leather chair while she sat on a straight chair a few feet away from him.

"Can I offer you any refreshment? Rosa can easily—."

"No, I am fine, thank you."

Laura noted his smile did not reach his eyes.

"So what can I do for you Mr. Davis?"

"The company I represent has heard of your wonderful research on dinosaurs, especially the Velociraptor and are quite knowledgeable of your veterinarian skills so they would like to offer you a position."

Laura looked at him blankly for a moment, her mind going back to another time and place. It had been a year since she had been on the island.

"Our company is new, just on its feet. We have a few animals in already so we would dearly love to have you on our team."

"What type of animal or animals will I be involved with?"

"It would involve mostly rare and endangered species."

"Your offer sounds intriguing but I will have to decline. I am quite happy where I am and have no desire to change right now."

For a moment Davis sat in silence. A small muscle in his lower jaw twitched as he spoke, "I am sorry to hear that you feel this way. Is there anything I can do that would help you change your mind?"

Laura suddenly felt the need for this man to leave. "No, there is nothing you can do. My mind is set. I thank you for the offer." With that Laura stood up, indicating to her guest the conversation was done. "Please allow me to show you to the door."

For a moment it seemed as though he wasn't going to move, but seeing that he wasn't going to gain anything more by pushing the point further he rose to his feet and allowed Laura to escort him to the door. As the door closed behind him he walked down the steps, over the sidewalk and got behind the driver's seat of a Mercury Marques. Adjusting his body in the seat and bringing his seat belt over his left shoulder to secure it beside his right thigh he started the car then allowed it to move forward.

"Always the safe driver."

Vince looked in the rear view mirror at the figure sitting in the shadow of the car's interior. Vince remained silent.

"I take it she did not accept our offer?"

Vince shook his head causing the man to sigh.

"We gave it our best shot. No need to worry though. There is always the option of showing her the benefits our offer can bring, especially when she experiences what we have to give. I know she won't pass it up the next time we approach her on the subject. For now we can work on our project, get things set up and ready. The first stage is complete, now onto the second." Leaning back against the car's seat he closed his eyes, thinking of his next step while Vince smiled in agreement.

❄ ❄ ❄ ❄ ❄

Sunlight sent shafts of light through the trees while flooding a small clearing where a small herd of Hadrosaurs grazed peacefully. Nearby a larger herd of Pentaceratops browsed, some even attempting to rest. A few heads turned when the lead bull suddenly bellowed, shaking his large bony frill and head in an attempt to intimidate his rival. Still not content he lowered his head and charged. The other bull met him head to head. With horns locked they spent the next few hours shoving and struggling. With time the rival weakens, its back bends and its hind legs take the strain. Soon his legs buckle, forcing him to retreat from the contest, leaving the lead bull as the undisputed leader of the herd.

Both herds soon settle back into their normal routines oblivious to the pair of eyes watching them from the forests edge. The alpha male Raptor came upon the power struggle thirty minutes before it ended. Now that the battle was over he watched the loser limp away. The thought of bringing him down had occurred but he knew better. Being alone he was no match for the five ton, twenty foot long beast with its long huge horns and large frill.

Moving away from the clearing he traveled for a distance, stopping when he sensed he was not alone. A soft breeze moved around bushes and past trees, offering him no clue as to the creature's identity. His muscles tensed, ready for flight if necessary, while his eyes searched for movement. Then, for what seemed like minutes dragging, but was only a few seconds the alpha female Raptor revealed herself, exiting from behind a nearby tree. Lowering her head toward him she emitted several clicking sounds as though she were chewing him out for startling her. Ignoring the response he walked over to her and they nudged each other in greeting. Once finished they moved off toward the safety of the pack. As they traveled the fresh sent of meat reached the alpha male. Pausing briefly he suddenly switched directions causing the mother raptor to stop and watch his retreating form. Not quite understanding why he moved away from the direction of home she followed. It was not long when she got a whiff of the delicious aroma and quickened her pace to match his.

Weaving around trees, fallen limbs, and huge rocks they finally saw what they were seeking, which caused the mother raptor to slow down. Something did not feel right as she faced a huge cage, one similar to what she had spent time in months ago. As she watched her mate enter and begin to eat nothing stirred, all was quiet, as though the land was holding its breath. She took a tentative step forward. Where was her two-legger companion and why did she remain hidden? Another step forward, then it hit her, so suddenly that at first it took her off guard…the scent of two-leggers, strangers to the land. Quickly she sent an alarm call to her mate, but not quick enough. Just as the alpha male wolfed down a mouthful of food and turned to look at her, the gate closed, bars suddenly separating them.

Forgetting his meal the alpha male turned his full attention on the gate as though it were a new enemy that challenged him. He screeched, and then charged, hitting the gate full force, which caused him to fall back, shaking his head. He then heard the soft clicking coming from the mother raptor. He watched her as she approached the cage in an attempt to calm him. They nudged as best they could between the bars. Neither one noticed the light in the far right corner of the cage as it flashed on, then off, then on.

Both stood close for up to half an hour when a sudden loud *whomp, whomp, whomp*, filled the air above them, followed by vegetation being whipped from side to side and debris, dirt and sand being tossed through the air. Both animals screeched, startled by the sudden change in their quiet world. The alpha male moved backward as though safety and security were in the rear of the cage while his mate turned, racing into the security of the nearby trees and bushes.

As the mother raptor reached the safety of the trees she turned to check on her mate. In the middle of the melee she caught the glint of metal from the sun's rays, drawing her gaze to the top of the cage. A huge hovering bird hung in the air a hundred feet above her mate's enclosure. Dangling from its underside was a crew of two-leggers. The rotors of the chopper set an even *whomp, whomp* as the men quickly hooked up the cage then shimmied up the rope. The mother raptor was impressed by their agility but this quickly passed as she saw the cage move up five hundred feet into the air. She could hear her mate screech in anger and fear, which caused her to follow the receding cage in an attempt to reach him. But this soon failed as the cage quickly disappeared behind the intertwining branches and leaves of the trees.

* * * * *

Bradley Sinclair sat at his desk in his office on West Bradford Street briefly reviewing the notes of the last meeting held thirty minutes ago and that his secretary, Mrs. Chandler had just finished typing. She was always one for detail; making sure things got done on schedule. Being five years his senior she, at all times appeared neatly dressed with her hair coifed in a professional manner. Mrs. Chandler was the epiphany of the efficient secretary.

Bradley was pleased with the detail of the notes and said so as he walked past Mrs. Chandler's desk, as well as wishing her a good day. Walking out into the hall of the twenty story building he approached one of several elevators. When the door opened he waited for two ladies and their dates to exit before he entered. Once inside he selected the lobby floor and relaxed a bit, watching the floor numbers descend. When the elevator reached its goal the doors opened allowing Bradley to view the main lobby complete with a high ceiling, a mirrored wall to the left, a few chairs, a receptionists desk near the right wall close to the front, three or four tall plants placed throughout the room, and a huge floor to ceiling glass window beside glass exit doors directly opposite of where he stood.

Turning sharply to the right he exited through a door to enter the parking ramp. Heading in the direction his car was parked he noted several other vehicles parked in other slots, some of which he recognized, a hatchback Chevy Aveo in pristine white, one Dodge Caravan in light blue, several types of trucks such as a Dodge Dakota, some older style working vans along with a dark blue Ford XLT Econoline and a beautiful Kia Optima in bright red. The one that stood out from them all was his, a Ford Fusian SE in brilliant silver.

One thing Bradley stuck to, being a businessman, and entrepreneur was a tight schedule and part of that schedule included getting home to his beautiful wife and son. The fact that there were quite a few vehicles still parked in their designated spaces told him he was on his perspective timetable. Leaving before rush hour traffic guaranteed a somewhat easier time of arriving home.

As he unlocked his car Bradley pushed the contents of the parking ramp out of his mind as he thought of spending time with his family. Tossing his brief case in the passenger side he felt a sharp sting just behind his shoulder, at the base of his neck. Thinking it was a mosquito he reached back, slapping the source of the puncture. He was shocked when he felt something metallic and cold. Puzzled he pulled it out and stared in disbelief at the small silver canister with its petite needle and hollow point, which allowed some type of drug to flow into his system. Shocked awareness of what he held hit him.

What! Why? Who would do this to him?

He turned to scan his surroundings, quickly taking note of two men wearing dark clothing coming from the Ford Econoline and carrying what appeared to be a body bag walking toward him. Panic seized him, causing him to lean back against the car as his balance wavered while, at the same time trying to reach his cell phone clipped to his belt. His fingers rebelled to his brain's commands as the drug started to take affect, feeling it course through his system. Bradley struggled, pushed by adrenaline he grasped the phone but his arm felt like lead, not wanting to respond. Whatever the drug was it was fast acting causing the numbness to spread, the phone slipping from his fingers.

His head leaned back against the car as his world began to spin in slow motion; images being strange, abnormal were now becoming dim and foggy. The men were closer now, changing into a cloud of ebony. He tried to speak, shout at them, curse them but his tongue felt heavy. In a last ditch effort to defend himself he tried to swing at them but his legs lost the struggle to hold his weight causing him to collapse onto the concrete floor as he sank into unconsciousness.

* * * * *

The mother raptor rested on a nest of eggs, listening to the early morning activity of a spring day. Dew hung heavy on blades of grass and leaves as the sun snaked small rays of light through the branches of the forest in an attempt to reach the dew while ascending into the sky. All was quiet now. After a successful hunt the pack tended to the nests, four for this season. Three other females resided on a nest while others slept nearby. Several of the males lolled around while some remained alert for possible danger. The hatchlings from last season were half grown being one year old and quite capable of contributing to the hunt.

As she watched her pack members the mother raptor took note of the young female the two-legger climber had protected from harm last season. The other females were submissive to the alpha, whereas this one showed the potential for leadership. By the next season the teenager would be a major competitor for the alphas role. Usually the mother raptor would attempt to chase her off as a potential threat but not this time. Things have changed. Her mate was gone, which was a given fact. Since alphas mate for life this was quite serious. She could choose another mate, which she has done in the past, or go in search of the one she lost. She chose the latter, but she did not know where to look. This was a problem too difficult for her to solve.

A few hours later she was traveling again with some of the pack. The time had come to hunt once again. Reaching a clearing similar to the one the alpha male had come across a few days ago the pack watched the movements of a large Hadrosaurus herd. Each Raptor searched for a specific member of the herd, one who was injured somehow, sick, or a young one. Once chosen the pack remnant set to work. First came the task of separating their target, in this case an older, slower member of the herd, from the rest of the group. Once done the initial attack began. Each Raptor had to work as a team since bringing down a four ton, forty foot long adult was no easy task. Two would distract the animal while another jumped on the Hadrosaur's back, digging into its flesh with long, taloned claws, ripping, slashing and tearing with the longer claw on the rear feet. The Hadrosaur bellowed in pain and terror in an effort to shake him free. Soon exhaustion was inevitable causing him to give up his struggle.

After the pack fed they left, heading back to the nesting site. As they traveled the mother raptor suddenly stopped. A familiar sound reached her ears. Emitting a soft clicking noise she moved toward the sound with her pack following.

A few minutes later the anticipation was overwhelming of solving her problem as the sound grew louder. So close, so close. Just on the other side of a small valley. The alpha female charged through the pass. Once she reached the other side anxiety set in as the *whomp, whomp, whomp* of the rotors fell away allowing the helicopter to fade out of sight, leaving silence in its wake. For a moment the mother raptor was disoriented, the silence overwhelming. When the scent reached her the alpha recognized it immediately, moving again in the direction of the pungent odor.

The cage stood in stark contrast against its surroundings of foliage and trees while the sun's light spread its shadow over the ground. As the Raptors arrived they stopped at the forests edge to stare at the cage suspiciously, each one uncertain of approaching, even though the smell of the meat was strong. Since each one had just fed they were able to resist the temptation allowing room for caution.

Because of the unusualness of the setting each member looked to their alpha for direction. The only one who was not affected by the scene was the mother raptor. She knew exactly what it was and had no problems in taking the lead. The only snag was the female teenager, who at the moment the alpha moved to investigate, so did she. Suddenly overcome with curiosity the teenager felt the need to inspect the strange but enticing creature, quickly forgetting her role in the pack, of which the mother raptor speedily reminded her of the error. Turning on the teenager she snapped a warning, nicking the youngster on the shoulder as she hissed loudly. The teenager jumped back, recovered quickly by arching her neck and snarled viciously at the alpha, challenging her. For a moment the mother raptor was astonished by the boldness of the young Raptor, but only for a moment. Charging at the youngster the alpha placed another small gash on her other shoulder and pushed her to the ground. Standing over the teenager she placed one seven inch scythe like claw over the youngster's mid-section. Leaning forward she hissed threateningly close to the teenager's face, quickly clearing up the issue of authority and placing a distinct boundary as to each one's position in the group.

The teenager froze, not daring to move for to do so would mean certain death. What seemed like an eternity, but only seconds she was released. Scrambling quickly to her feet she moved to where the rest of the pack stood, her cuts stinging reminders of her defeat.

Turning away from the scene the alpha approached the cage, showing no fear. The faint scent of her mate still lingered as well as the very prominent odor of two-leggers. Ignoring the latter while delighting in her mate's scent she walked into the cage.

＊ ＊ ＊ ＊ ＊

Laura sat in the nursery watching Jayden play with some blocks while waiting for Bradley to come home. She had just arrived home fifteen minutes ago after a long day in the zoo's clinic. Even though she was in a managerial role, complete with the position's duties she still kept up with things in the clinic. Today her session at the gym with her friend Jill was replaced with some extended hours. Once finished Laura's thoughts were on her son and the fact she missed him, wanting to spend quality time with him. Jill understood since she was also a mother. After arriving home she paid the babysitter for the days work, checked with Rosa on supper, and then went to the nursery where Jayden, at that time was sleeping.

Since Jayden was now playing quietly Laura took some time to browse through a magazine she had received in the mail. It was not surprising she jumped when her cell phone rang. She glanced at the number and frowned.

"Hello?"

"Yes hello. I am looking for a Mrs. Sinclair."

"I am Mrs. Sinclair."

"My name is Bernard Sanchez and I represent the Costa Rican government. It has been brought to our attention by one of the fishermen who fish in the area of Isle Angusti Don that some suspicious activity has been going on there and we are wondering if you are aware of this."

In other words they were actually wondering if the zoo was responsible. "No. What kind?"

"It seems that some fishermen saw one helicopter fly over the island, hover for a bit, then take off carrying a cage. They were pretty sure the animal inside was a Raptor. Did the zoo change its mind…?"

"I don't know who has done this or why but I assure you that the San Diego Zoo was not responsible."

"Okay Mrs. Sinclair. If you should find out who has taken the animal please tell them they need to return it immediately. Sorry to have bothered you."

"No problem."

After hanging up Laura decided to take Jayden to play on the porch while she waited for Bradley and puzzled over Sanchez's words. Who in their right mind would take Raptors from the island? Sitting Jayden on a blanket with some of his toys Laura sat in a patio chair once again attempting to browse through her magazine while her mind searched for an explanation concerning the Raptor theft.

A few minutes later she was eating supper while helping Jayden eat. All the while she wondered what was keeping her husband. She was only mildly worried as he sometimes ended up being late, even though he thrived on a tight schedule. Once done she left the dining room and entered the family room to enjoy some television time. Placing Jayden in his playpen she sat on a nearby sofa. With remote in hand she scanned the stations settling for an Alfred Hitchcock movie. Settling comfortably she got out her cell and dialed Bradley's personal number. It quickly went to voicemail.

Two hours later, as the credits played Laura noted that her son had fallen asleep. Switching off the TV she picked up Jayden, carried him up to his room and placed him in his crib. As he slept she changed his clothes and diaper. He was a sound sleeper and only moaned slightly as she placed his tiny body in certain positions. Finishing up she covered him, placed a kiss on his forehead and left the room. While Jayden slept she busied herself around the house, trying to push her growing anxiety to the side. Stopping briefly on the Sundeck she looked out at the night, watching the darkness spreading across the land as night time took control. It was now close to the nine o'clock hour. Again she took out her cell to dial Bradley's number and once more it went to voicemail. Something was wrong, very wrong.

Walking back into the family room she walked over to the left side of the room where a desk took up a major part. She quickly located the phone number for the local police and picked up the land phone to dial.

"Mistress Laura?"

Laura looked up to see Rosa, a worried expression on her face.

"There are two police officers here to see you."

Laura quickly left the room to greet the officers, puzzled as to why they were here. As she approached them standing in the open foyer Laura took in their appearance. Each wore crisp blue uniforms, clean and pressed. Their weapon belts and shoes were cleaned and shined. Both stood with legs wide, one foot back, chest out, back straight, arms out with hands free. The female officer was slim, at least five feet, seven inches tall with long blond hair tied back in a bun. Her partner was a few inches taller, broad shouldered with an athletic build. His hair was cut short as though he had come from the military. Their somber facial expressions told Laura this was not going to be good.

"Mrs. Sinclair? I'm Officer Rick Garrett and my partner, Officer Tessa McKenzie. We are with the Central division and are following up on a report of an abandoned vehicle. A call came in from a Ms. Chandler—."

"That is my husband's secretary."

"—that a Ford Fusion SE, belonging to a Mr. Bradley Sinclair was still parked in its stall on West Broadway Street as she left for the day. Ms. Chandler became concerned because Mr. Sinclair had left twenty minutes before."

Laura gasped. "What has happened to him?"

"We are following up on that now ma'am," spoke McKenzie. My partner and I wanted to check in with you to see if he had arrived home by another means, such as with a fellow colleague or friend?"

"No, he is not here." Laura felt her world was about ready to collapse. She barely heard Officer Garrett speak again, her mind racing for answers.

"Would he have left with anyone to meet somewhere for drinks, maybe just unwind a little before coming home?"

"If there is one thing about my husband I do know is that he is very devoted to his family. He would not go out with friends and not tell me!"

Both officers did not flinch at her statement, each hearing this type of response before. Officer Garrett decided to continue. "Have you or your husband been threatened or harassed by anyone?"

"No. My husband just did not disappear by himself, someone took him!"

"Why do you come to this conclusion?"

Laura looked at Officer Garrett as though he were lacking serious intelligence. "Because he is not home where he should be, which is with his wife and son!"

"Okay Mrs. Sinclair. We will still continue to investigate and will keep you informed. Just in case you get a ransom call we would like to put a bug on your phone so as to trace the call."

"That would be fine, and thank you!"

Both officers nodded in agreement and left. Closing the door behind them and locking it Laura walked up to her son's room. For awhile she watched his sleeping form. It gave her comfort. Focusing on Jayden and how much he is like his father kept her from dwelling on the fact that she would not have the comforting arms of Bradley this night. There would be no sleep for her tonight.

* * * * *

Sun had spread over the vast expanse of land, staining everything it touched a bright rosy pink. All of this went unnoticed by Laura as she sat in the kitchen watching Rosa prepare breakfast. As she waited Laura worked at helping Jayden eat some cereal. The scents of fresh toast, scrambled eggs, and sausage filled the room causing Laura's stomach to turn traitor. The aroma teased her system, telling her it was time to eat while her heart and mind rebelled. Her husband was missing. There was nothing she could do except wait on the police and the justice system. How could she think about eating, especially as Rosa placed a plate of food in front of her?

"Mistress Laura? Don't worry so. The police will find him. Now you eat. You need to keep your strength up, if not for yourself then for your precious little boy."

Laura looked at Jayden as he tried putting cereal in his mouth by using his hand. She smiled, picking up his spoon to give to him. "Thank you Rosa, I will try."

After breakfast Laura started getting ready for work. Part of her wanted to stay home but she knew better. It was important for her to keep busy. After the babysitter arrived and was comfortably with Jayden in his room Laura went down the steps toward the garage. When she got to the baker's pantry the doorbell sounded. Quickly passing through the dining room and into the open foyer she opened the door, thinking it was the police with some good news. When she opened it she came face-to-face with Vince Davis. Her countenance fell, disappointment evident on her face. This did not bother Davis. "Good morning Mrs. Sinclair."

Laura quickly composed herself. "Mr. Davis, this really is not a good time and I have not changed my mind from our previous conversation."

"I assure you I won't be long. My employer wishes to ask if you would consider helping us out."

"If this is another job offer I am not interested."

"It is not exactly a job per se."

Laura frowned as Davis continued.

"My employer wishes to retrieve something of value on one of the dinosaur islands. He had attempted to send a team in but they were attacked by a dinosaur before they had gotten out."

Laura stared at him as the enormity of what he was saying sunk in. "How can one small individual such as me go in to get this object when a team of men could not? What makes me so unique?"

"You will not exactly be alone. My employer is very knowledgeable of your time you spent on Isle Angusti Don with the Raptors because of your research. For this reason he has acquired an adult Raptor for you to train and take with you."

Laura couldn't believe what she was hearing. She then remembered the helicopter. "Your employer was the one who is responsible for taking one of the Raptors off of the second island!"

"Actually we have two."

"Two! These types of animal are still creatures of habit. They should be returned to their natural habitat. Keeping them where people coexist is not a good idea!"

"I am sure my employer will keep that in mind."

"Well I highly suggest you put them back. I also cannot help you at this time so if you will excuse me I am quite late for work."

Closing the door she turned, walking back through the dining room toward the garage. Laura did not get far when she heard the doorbell ring again.

"Now what is it?" She turned again to retrace her steps to the door and opening it found no one was there. Puzzled she was about to close the door again when her peripheral vision saw the small box sitting on the porch floor. Picking it up she saw the small envelope attached. Opening it first she read the short note inside. 'Please be ready to leave at ten a.m. A car will stop to pick you up.'

Totally stumped by the note Laura opened the box. As she looked inside her mouth fell open and her eyes grew round. In the bottom of the box sat her husband's cell phone and car keys. For a moment she seemed frozen in place as she took the objects into her mind, realizing the impact of what they represented. Jerking herself into action she looked at her watch. She had an hour and thirty minutes.

Going back into the house she started up the stairs while dialing Jill's number. Her friend answered on the second ring.

"Hey Jill, this is Laura."

"Hi, are we still on for next weeks climbing adventure?"

"I may have to postpone. Right now I need to ask a favor of you. Can you meet me at my place, say in ten minutes?"

"Sure, what's up?"

"I will explain when you get here."

By the time Laura hung up she was in the master bedroom. Getting her duffle bag she began to pack a few things. Once done she went to the nursery. Jayden was still asleep while the babysitter sat nearby, using her laptop. She looked up when Laura entered the room. At seventeen Cindy Conner took her job seriously, always staying close to her charges. Because of this her babysitting skills were highly sought by parents through the agency Cindy worked for. Seeing her new employer the agency assigned to her come back suddenly worried her, making her doubt herself.

"Is everything all right Mrs. Sinclair?"

"Everything is fine Cindy. I have just had a sudden change in my plans and will have to leave town for a few days. I am arranging to have my friend Jill take care of Jayden for me because I am not sure when I will be back. I will pay you for the next two weeks worth of wages since this came up so suddenly and was not your fault."

Laura took the time then to write Cindy a check and gave it to her.

"Thank you Mrs. Sinclair. If your friend needs some assistance please have her call me. I will be happy to help."

"That will be fine."

Collecting her things Cindy left. Laura walked over to the crib to look at her son. He looked so peaceful. Bending over him she planted a kiss on his forehead.

"I will bring your father home," she whispered. "I promise."

A few minutes later Jill arrived. Laura explained things the best she could with the time she had. Jill agreed to take care of Jayden but did not like the idea of Laura going by herself.

"Laura, I think you should tell the police. This sounds very fishy to me. How do you know that they really have Bradley? It could be a gimmick."

"I don't think so and I don't have time to call the police and please don't call them. They would want me to stick around to answer questions and I have no time."

Both women jumped at the sound of a car horn.

"There is my ride to the airport. Don't worry Jill. Everything will work out, I know it will."

Jill shook her head as she watched Laura leave the house and climb into the back seat of a Mercury Marquee.

* * * * *

By eight that evening Rosa Chavez arrived home, a single level apartment on the bottom floor just three blocks from where Laura and Bradley live. The building was large, holding at least seven other apartments above them while offering plenty of living space. This fit very well for Rosa and her seventeen year old son Ramon.

As Rosa entered the living room she could hear music coming from her son's room. She was glad to know he was home and safe but she was not surprised. Knowing him he was at his computer programming a game or hacking into something he should not while other teenagers his age were partying and dating.

Entering the kitchen she prepared a quick meal for the both of them. When finished she called Ramon. In a short time he entered the kitchen, grabbed his plate of food and milk, then left. Rosa smiled. Not even a hello, thank you or goodbye. She did not mind because she understood his motives. Each shared their tender moments while respecting each others privacy. Rosa also knew that her son was grow-ing into a young man and, even though she knew communication was important for their relationship; her son's independence was just as necessary.

As she ate her meal thoughts of Mistress Laura and her sud-den exodus from the house this morning filled her mind. When Jill informed her of the reason why Laura left in a hurry she immediately wanted to call the police. Jill agreed. By the time two officers from the Western division came to take Jill's statement it was already too late to locate Laura. Even so the officers made an attempt to check the airport. The two officers were not happy, stressing the point that Laura should have informed them immediately upon being contacted by the kidnappers. The two officers left shortly after, stating that they would connect with the two officers from the Central division to fill them in. Now all anyone could do was to wait.

After she finished eating Rosa cleaned the dishes and straightened up the kitchen. Walking down a short hall to her bedroom she noted Ramon's light was still on. Knocking gently she opened the door to look inside. On first impression she noted his room in slight disarray, which was not his normal. When this happened it usually meant he was engrossed in trying to solve a particular problem, either online or a programming issue related to his job. Rosa was proud of her son for landing a very lucrative job in designing video games. At first she was leery of it for fear his school grades would suffer but he reassured her that he could make it work. He explained things to his employer and he gave Ramon part time hours until after he graduated in a couple of months. Even so, between his job and school her son was kept pretty busy, which left those in between moments for his favorite hobby of hacking. Silently closing the door she went down to her own room to sleep.

Ramon heard the knock and knew his mom was checking on him. He did not mind this, knowing it gave his mom peace of mind. The one stable part of his life has been his mother since his father had left before he was born. He had struggled quite a bit during his early teens. Being like most teenagers he had experimented with drugs and alcohol. Fortunately it did not last long. At the age of sixteen he learned the consequences of such a life in cold reality. Two of his friends, along with their girlfriends were on their way home from a party and drove into the other lane colliding head on with a semi. All four had died. Two things hit home concerning the accident. First was the fact they were drunk while driving, which was the reason the accident happened, and second, he could have easily been with them. A fluke had prevented him from going. He had passed out on the couch.

From that point on he began to try different kinds of hobbies to express his individuality. Through time he developed a system of values and the highlight was the discovery of programming, which spread to his favorite hobby of hacking. His mother supported and guided him in his decisions, realizing he was struggling for his independence and freedom as a young adult. There were, of course some rules he had to follow, such as helping around the house, keeping his room tidy and because of his job, pay some of the bills. He also saw the need to have good contact with his mother, knowing that communication was the key. The only area he failed in this was when he experimented with drugs and alcohol. That part of his life was an embarrassment for him and there was no reason his mother should know of it. What was in the past should stay in the past.

He was pleased with the direction his life was going now, especially concerning his hobby. The world of the hacker is full of fascinating problems waiting to be solved. There was a basic thrill from solving these problems while sharpening his programming skills and exercising his intelligence. Because of this he was never bored or laboring for nothing, especially if the work was repetitive. One who is able to think should never be forced into a situation that bores him?

Being a hacker also gave him freedom to solve whatever problem he was fascinated by so he ignored anyone who told him he could not find a solution. His competence as a hacker involved practice, dedication, intelligence, and hard work. These accomplishments were vital to him as a hacker.

Staring at his computer monitor Ramon looked over the game program he had been working on. Deciding it would do for now he saved it then closed his program. From there he went to his favorites list to select a special website. He then noted the clock on the wall above him. In thirty minutes he would be able to view an actual fight between two dinosaurs. He was quite impressed with the web site, having accidentally finding it while doing research earlier for his game program, and that it was password protected. This offered him a new problem, locating the password. He was all to willing to meet the challenge of creatively overcoming an obstacle, especially since he was curious over the contents of the site. He felt confident with his decision since it went along with one of his two basic principles, which was the belief that system cracking for fun and exploitation is ethically okay as long as the cracker commits no theft, vandalism or breach of confidentiality. He was just curious.

While approaching the problem he discovered that he could not get past the opening 'password required' box. To go past that problem he did a WHOIS Lookup for the site. Once he found the host and its IP address he launched Web Snake using the IP address. This resulted in a mirror of the entire server.

In order to speed things up a bit and preventing a lot of files and images Ramon did not need he set Web Snake to not download anything over 20k. Even with this shortcut the process took a long time so Ramon set it for the evening before bed time and let it run while he slept. By morning, which ended up being on a Saturday he had an image of the entire server. Looking through the listed directories he found one listed as /clashingdinos. Opening that directory all the contents, including the sub-directories were an open book. Locating the index page he copied it, and then pasted it in a web browser, clicked 'enter' and he was on the site. To keep it he saved it to his favorites.

After saving it he took his first long look at the site. He noted the two dinosaurs to fight were a Torvosaurus and an Allosaurus. Both were large carnivores. The Allosaurus weighed in at four tons, thirty-five feet long from nose to tail and, standing upright was sixteen and a half feet tall. The Torvosaurus weighed in at six tons, thirty-six feet long and ten feet tall. Ramon thought they were pretty evenly matched. The time of the fight was to be at ten p.m.

Two other parts of the website really puzzled him. First he noted a link that read: "Special Guests." This gained him access to a form with strict instructions that allowed him to attend an actual fight. This he brushed off as a hoax, not bothering to read any more. Second there were people placing bets and he could not understand why if the fight was not real? Now, as he sat waiting for the show to start he saw the bidding had gone up to an extreme amount.

Five minutes before the show began words scrolled across the site reminding bidders that betting ended promptly in four minutes. As the minutes ticked away the message became bolder. At ten sharp bidding closed and the video screen opened up.

At first nothing moved as the camera focused on lush green vegetation, an open area, almost like a field surrounded by trees. Ramon jumped when the Allosaurus appeared, walking toward the center of the arena. Shaking its head he looked around as though seeing the area for the first time. The sound of a bellowing roar told the Allosaurus he was not alone. Charging toward him at full speed was a bull Torvosaurus. He had little time to react but it was enough. Being more agile he quickly moved to the side allowing the momentum of Torvo's charge to pass him but not before he turned, sinking his four inch teeth into the Torvo's left thigh, ripping out a chunk of flesh. The Torvo roared in pain and anger while turning to face the Allosaurus. Bending down low and arching its neck the Torvo roared again, showing long terrifying teeth, intending to intimidate. The Allosaurus stood his ground, swishing his tail from side to side and flexing his seven inch claws. His jaws opened slightly as his nostrils filled with the scent of blood. His anticipation intensified as he sensed a kill while his eyes missed nothing. As the Torvo charged again the Allosaurus saw the Torvo favor his hurt leg.

The Allosaurus quickly stepped to the side as the Torvo charged him. He knew when the Torvo stepped on his injured leg he saw him unconsciously move his head to the right. That was the opening the Allosaurus sought. It was a fraction moment and his timing had to be right. When the moment came he took it, clamping his jaws tight onto the back of the Torvo's neck, just behind the skull while the seven inch claws swept in a downward motion flaying the flesh just behind the shoulder. Bringing his right foot up the Allosaurus sliced at the Torvo's stomach while using the momentum to push the Torvo off balance. When the Torvo landed on its side the Allosaurus moved to pin him down. The Torvo shuddered then lay still. Releasing him the Allosaurus moved in to feast, tearing chunks of flesh off, swallowing them whole as the video dimmed, then turned black.

Ramon was awestruck. He was impressed over the realistic effects of the fight and the animation involved. A minute later the web site scrolled the results declaring the victor to be the Allosaurus. Then it stated that betting would resume in ten minutes for the next fight between a Velociraptor, a human being and a Nanotyrannus. The time was Sunday at ten p.m., tomorrow. Ramon stared at the word human-being thinking, *No way!* Now he knew the videos were computer generated animation because people were not around during that time. Ramon knew he would be up to watch. This was one fight he did not want to miss.

* * * * *

Bradley groaned as he began to wake up. Every muscle in his body seemed to ache. As his mind became active he became more aware of his surroundings. At first he could not remember much but the feeling quickly left as thoughts of his kidnapping flooded his mind. His eyes flew open and he sat straight up, unconsciously swinging his feet over the edge of his cot. The sudden movement caused his head to spin making him stop for a moment to get his bearings. Rubbing the tension from his temples he allowed his eyes to focus, taking in the details of his immediate area. The sight did not appeal to him. He was sectioned off from the rest of a huge room by steel bars extending from floor to ceiling. His cage was divided as he could vaguely make out another dark, shadowed cage to his left, with a small access door. Outside of the cage he noted one door to his right and another on the proceeding wall possibly six feet away from the first door. Moving his gaze to look straight ahead he saw three rows of seats placed as though they were in a theater and in front of them, extending close to the full length of the opposite wall was a window. Looking through the window he could see a large open area of land surrounded by trees. What was behind the trees puzzled him. Extending just above the tops of the trees and branching out in a half circle was a wall. It reminded Bradley of an arena, although this one seemed camouflaged.

Standing up Bradley walked on shaky legs to the bars outlining his enclosure. Grabbing one of them he could feel how cold and final it was. Shaking it hard he sensed they were solidly based. Nothing would budge them. It also helped to shake a little of the frustration off that he was feeling. Walking back over to the cot he sat down, suddenly feeling quite tired. Laying his head on the small pillow he closed his eyes, oblivious to the pair of eyes watching him.

* * * * *

The mother raptor lay in the far shadowed corner of her cage resting. The only time she moved was to watch the two-legger. She had been there awhile since a couple of two-leggers dragged him in. After they left she walked over to him, curiosity getting the better of her. His scent was familiar. She recognized him as the climber's mate.

A few moments later he began to move. She remained quiet as she observed him waking up to realize he was also held inside this small enclosure. When he returned to his rest area the mother raptor decided to sleep as well.

* * * * *

As Laura followed Mr. Davis from the helicopter pad she wondered what kind of business his employer was involved in. The building she was approaching was beautifully designed in a very deep brown and cream shade. It was obvious the architect knew what he was doing. The main entrance extended out in the fashion of a large bay window. In the center was the door designed in a dark colored wood. Above them was a sign that said 'Welcome to Isle Ebony.'

Walking through the entrance Laura was met with a breath-taking view of design. She had obviously stepped into some kind of a lobby, one that was quite huge. A chandelier hung from the ceiling, sending tiny prisms of light throughout the room. The floor was done in tile of a light tan but ended to her right with a plush cream carpet. Resting on that was two dark brown couches facing each other and a smaller couch with its back to her in an attempt to form a U-shape. This U-shape allowed the fake burning embers of a fire to spread its artificial warmth toward the couches. The manufactured flames were surrounded by a black fireplace.

Laura's gaze swept the enclosure, taking note of the scenic pictures framed in that same dark colored wood lining the walls. Her gaze stopped at the windows where a small ebony wood table and two chairs sat. The contents on top of the table quickly drew her to its side. A chessboard displaying all sixteen chess pieces, half a very deep brown and the other half in black stood on their assigned squares. All had a glossy sheen. What impressed Laura were the shapes of the pieces. Each piece was intricately carved into the shape of a dinosaur. The T-Rex took the place of the king, the queen being the Allosaurus, the bishop was the Spinosaurus, the knight being the Megalosaurus, the castle was the Edmarka Rex, and the pawns were the popular Velociraptor. The set was quite impressive.

Laura was so intent on her perusal of the room that she did not see Vince leave and someone else enter a few minutes later. When she heard a different voice she jumped.

"They are quite beautiful pieces of art. I call them Ebony in Action."

Laura turned at the sound and gasped, her eyes growing round in shock and surprise as she took an involuntary step back. He ignored her reaction, continuing on.

"This type of dark colored wood comes from trees of tropical and warm regions and is so versatile. It can be transferred into anything and everything. There are so many uses, each bringing out its own kind of beauty. Its shine and texture doesn't diminish over time."

"But….but you are dead!"

Now the man turned from admiring the chess pieces to look directly at Laura. "No, I am very much alive. But my twin brother is dead, no thanks to you."

* * * * *

Bradley lay still, sensing that something was wrong, especially when he heard someone moving about. Slowly he opened an eye, then another. Without moving his head he allowed his eyes to scan his immediate area. Other than the small door being open that separated his cage from the other, there was nothing out of the ordinary. All seemed still and quiet. Feeling that his imagination was getting the better of him he decided to ignore it. Stretching he moved to sit up. He stiffened when he felt something warm with his feet. Bradley knew the cot was large according to the normal design settings and had plenty of room to move freely about, so why were his feet connecting with something solid. He pulled his feet away while leaning up on his left elbow he looked at the foot of the cot. His eyes grew round, finding it suddenly difficult to breathe as he looked at the

Raptor resting peacefully just inches from his feet. He had no way of knowing that, during the night he had started tossing and turning in his sleep while emitting soft moaning noises. This alerted the mother raptor and her motherly instincts kicked in. Once she settled down near him he ceased his turning and tossing. Now, as Bradley moved she started making soft clicking sounds.

Bradley's fear suddenly abated as he heard the familiar noise causing him to frown, viewing the Raptor in a new light. This could not be the Raptor that had been at the zoo, could it? How did she get here and where were they exactly? The questions went unanswered as both heads turned at the sound of a door opening then closing. Bradley's eyes narrowed suspiciously at the approaching figure while the Raptor no longer purred.

Davis could not believe his eyes, stopping briefly to digest what he actually saw. The scene in the cage was not what he expected to see. He would have to inform his employer after he finished his task. Ignoring the stares he received Davis walked to the side of the cage containing the Raptor's empty nest. Opening the package he held Davis took out the piece of meat, and then tossed it into the cage. The mother raptor got up, smelling the meat and blood. Walking over to the divider bars she hesitated, the scene reminding her of another, very resent time. Her hesitation did not sit well with Davis.

"Great, what is the matter with you now? Fine have it your way." With that Davis reached inside his coat withdrawing a pistol, aiming it at the Raptor. Bradley saw the weapon and acted instinctively by jumping up to shout, "No!" This caused the mother raptor to step back thinking she should not go forward. She barely felt the small prick of a needle in the fatty part of her neck. In a matter of minutes she lay asleep on the floor of the cage.

"No need to get so irate Sinclair. It's just a dart gun."

Bradley was quite agitated now as he observed the calm attitude of his antagonist, which added fuel to the fire. His lips blade thin, cords on the back of his neck pronounced, he looked as if he were trying, and failing, to rein in his temper.

"You bastard! What the hell are you trying to prove? By whose authority are you doing this?"

"That would be my employer."

"Employer be damned!"

"Now, now, Mr. Sinclair, you won't accomplish anything by loosing your temper. Now, if you would be so kind as to step aside so the men can move the Raptor. She is going on a little trip."

Bradley reluctantly did as he was told as he saw Davis aim the dart pistol at him. He quietly sat on the cot watching several men dressed in maintenance uniforms remove the Raptor. As they left Davis followed them to the door.

"Tell your boss that I look forward to meeting him."

The threat was set. Davis turned to look at Sinclair who now stood close to the bars. Davis smiled, which rarely occurred. "Oh you will meet him shortly. You can count on it."

Then Bradley was alone.

* * * * *

Laura stared at the spitting image of her former boss, Jeff Thatcher. The same light blue eyes that looked like glass with pupils that reminded one of a reptile returned her stare with malicious intent as he stated his thoughts, feelings and intentions. Laura could do nothing but listen.

"I really miss my little brother, he being the youngest by only five minutes. We were always very close, doing things together, until our parents were killed in a car accident. Being ten at the time Jeff and I were immediately placed in foster care. Then the fight began. They wanted to separate us and we would have nothing to do with it. We lost the battle, each of us were adopted by different couples. Both of us made a pact before we were split apart to keep our birth names and to search for each other the first chance we got. We were able to connect again years later and since our lives were lived in different locations we kept in constant touch. My goodness, where are my manners. Please let us sit down. We have quite a bit to discuss. Oh and my name is Jim but most just call me J.T."

Taking Laura by the elbow he escorted her to one of the soft couches while he sat on the arm of another. Laura sat on its edge as though ready to take flight if needed, even though there was no where she could run.

"Now where was I—oh yes, Jeff would often spend the weekends. When he arrived it was always a special time. They were the greatest. Our days were spent out in the field hunting, the nights partying, enjoying each others company while catching up on the years missed. During this time Jeff would start discussing you and the feelings he had. I couldn't see why he was so interested in you, until now. Then you had to spoil it by marrying that creep Sinclair."

With the mention of Bradley Laura suddenly found her voice. "You took Bradley—why?"

"Mostly to get your attention because I really need your assistance and figured you would not willingly volunteer."

"You are quite correct. I was told by your employee of the task you want me to do. I thought he was crazy. When I realized he was serious I realized he is crazy."

J.T. smiled. Not only beautiful he thought, but quick-witted as well. "Then you know about the raptors." Her silence was enough to affirm his statement. "My reasons are simple. I later realized you would not have time to train a Raptor so I tried to find the one you were in close contact with. That is the only motive I had for taking them off their island."

At the sound of a door opening both looked to see who came in. Seeing that it was Davis J.T. got up to meet him. Standing a few feet from Laura they talked in a low monotone. Laura was only able to pick up bits and pieces of the conversation. "She is ready to go… what…really…she did…resilient bastard…very good then…"

A minute later J.T. returned, smiling as he sat back down. "Well I think it is time to set some ground rules. As you already know I need to gain access to a certain item encased in a bag located on the first island. The team I had sent in was attacked before they could get off the island and all were killed. Because of this I had to rethink my strategy. Since the team was visible to predators as a result of their number I came to the conclusion of using something less obvious. A dinosaur in amongst other dinosaurs and one person camouflaged with a dinosaurs scent, you can just picture the Trojan horse."

"Along with Davis I feel you would fit well with the insane."

J.T. glared at her, riveting her with his eyes. "Do this for me… Laura and I will return your husband to you."

Laura knew she had no choice. She would do anything to get Bradley back to her and Jayden, and this man facing her knew that. Bradley was her light and her life. She could not think of a world without him. "All right, I will do it. I suppose you would know the location of the bag."

"Yes of course. The team was in radio contact up to the point of the attack. We could easily pinpoint their location from that. You will be flown in via helicopter. The area is too overgrown with trees and bushes, making it impossible for the helicopter to land so it will allow you to be lowered in the nearest clearing. I would advise you, the moment you land to seek cover immediately."

"What is in this bag?"

"Let's just say it is something I desperately need."

In less than an hour Laura was again in the helicopter heading for the first island. Before taking off she was blindfolded but once in the air she was allowed to see again. During the time she was blindfolded she felt the helicopter take on another load of some kind. Once the blindfold was removed she forgot about it, getting totally immersed in the scene of the ocean spread out before her to be replaced shortly after with rocks, bushes, and trees of the first island. Passing a huge clearing she was able to see herds of dinosaurs grazing or milling about. A short way from there the helicopter located a small clearing. As the helicopter hovered Laura prepared to disembark by checking her supplies including the only weapon she was given, a huge knife.

The moment Laura touched ground she ran for the trees, barely catching a glimpse of an empty cage. Reaching the protection of the forest she stopped to look back, making sure of what she actually saw. The empty cage confirmed that the Raptor was also here. Now she had to decide if she should call to it or try and reach the bag on her own. Suddenly hearing the soft clicking sound from behind her said enough. The choice had been made.

Turning around to face the animal Laura recognized her immediately. Relief coursed through her, abruptly remembering there were other raptors on this island even though J.T. assured her they were on the other side.

The mother raptor approached Laura, greeting her happily by rubbing against her. Laura returned the greeting while clicking softly with her tongue. It was good to see her friend again

Once the greetings were finished Laura knew it was time to go. She had the route written out and double checking them again set off traveling in a southern direction. The mother raptor watched her move away, not understanding why. Laura noted her hesitation and stopped. Reaching for her backpack she found the picture of the bag she requested from J.T. Showing it to the Raptor Laura stated, "Find, we must find." Then Laura nodded her affirmation and the Raptor copied her, understanding. Putting the picture away and placing her backpack on, Laura moved off. The alpha female did not hesitate in following.

J.T. assured Laura the site was just a mile from the drop off point. She figured the Raptor was with her for protection so she stayed close to the female. Passing through a ravine, around several rock formations and through a stand of trees they reached their goal. Greeting them now was a larger clearing than the one they had just left.

On the opposite side a wall of rock faced them, forming a wide u-shape, covered with splotches of greenery. From small to large rocks were strewn about on the ground. In amongst them were a couple of trees growing tall, branches reaching to the sky while the bottom part had been stripped of its leaves by an herbivore. A fallen tree lay in pieces on the ground, obviously having been struck by lightening. The ground, reaching out to where they stood had been trampled down by a herd of plant eaters, evidently not long ago.

Laura was confused. This was the area she was to look for the bag but there were no matching landmarks to guide her. She suddenly felt very uneasy. The mother raptor sensed her agitation, gently nudging her. The abruptness of the move goaded her to action. Moving to her right she followed along the edge of the clearing until she reached the cliff. Moving along its base she began to search.

After a good thirty minutes she was totally frustrated and ready to call it quits. Either they had taken a wrong turn somehow or the bag was not here to begin with. It would be just like J.T. to send her on a wild goose chase.

Deciding to take a short break before heading back Laura rested near the base of one of the huge rocks. It was at that point she noted a distinct change in the mother raptor. Her posture tensed as she lifted her head to smell the air. Turning suddenly toward Laura the Raptor nudged her toward a safe crevice of rock. It had been so quiet and peaceful in the clearing that the sudden sound of a bellowing roar made Laura jump. The female Raptor turned to face her adversary.

* * * * *

Miles away Ramon sat transfixed as he started to watch his second fight. This fight he was definitely recording, using his video capture software. Seeing the animals face each other he quickly took note of their strengths and weaknesses. He did not; at that time see a person present.

* * * * *

Laura, on the other hand was not pleased with what she saw. Facing the female Raptor was a Nanotyrannus, often referred to as a tiny tyrant. For a while it was thought to be a juvenile since it was just third the size of a T-Rex, and part of the tyrannosaurid family. Later research indicated that the scull bones were fused, making it into an adult specimen. Other factors that defined the Nano's difference were the shape of the head and the bite pressure. The T-Rex could crush bone whereas the Nano could not. Now Laura could actually see the adult version in action.

As both animals faced each other Laura attempted to compare their sizes. First looking at them both it was very evident that the Nano was slightly larger than the mother raptor. The Nano looked to be eight feet tall where she knew the Raptor to be six and a half feet tall, a difference of one and a half feet. Their length, Laura estimated the Nano at sixteen feet and the Raptor she knew to be five feet, a difference of eleven feet. Their weight might be the key. She could tell the Nano was the heaviest, at least a ton, and the mother raptor, with a good two hundred pounds. That was a huge difference of eighteen hundred pounds. The weight of the Nano might be to the raptors advantage. Laura wished she could remember the Nano's fighting tactics.

Right now both were trying to sound intimidating by hissing and screeching. Laura took a sharp intake of breath as the Nano suddenly charged forward; delivering a quick bite attack to the Raptor's left side, and then turning abruptly for another. A quick turn on the Raptor's part prevented her from getting a duplicate bite on her right side. She struck out at the passing Nano with her right leg, her seven inch claw aiming for a leg but the Nano quickly side-stepped, darting in again to inflict another bite. The mother raptor saw him coming and bit down onto the Nano's left shoulder, not letting go. A loud bellow of pain echoed over the land.

Laura was dumbfounded. The Nano was not an opponent to underestimate. She was also becoming fearful, wishing the mother raptor was not alone. But....she was not alone. Quickly reaching for her backpack she began searching through its contents. She did not like weapons so refused to wear it on her belt. Seeing it now in its protective sheath she grabbed it. With knife in hand she looked at the fight, waiting.

She did not have long to hold back. The moment the Nano bellowed he came down with his huge narrow head, ramming the mother raptor, causing her to release the Nano's shoulder and knocking her off balance. Now that the Raptor was down the Nano moved in. This was Laura's chance as the end result left the Nano's back facing her. Leaving the safety of the rock a memory of her childhood years living on her father's horse ranch and the many times she had practiced vaulting onto the back of a horse until it was second nature for her flashed through her mind, but onto the back of a dinosaur? Well there was a first time for everything. Placing the knife between her teeth she ran toward the Nano. Her only problem was the tail.

The Nano, having reached his goal, moved in to give the lethal bite, which resulted in a slight lowering of the tail. It was enough for

Laura, the exact opening she needed. As the Nano lowered his head Laura landed on its back. To anchor herself she dug her heals into the Nano's ribcage and reached her left arm around its neck. Reaching for the knife with her right hand she arched her hand back to strike.

At first contact the Nano was baffled as to the sudden weight on his back. Glancing over his right shoulder he saw the source, anger surging through him just as a sharp pain coursed through his neck followed quickly by another. Bellowing loudly he swung his head back to strike. Laura saw the enormous jaws coming at her with sharp teeth covered in blood. Recoiling back from striking a third time she quickly let go, rolling off the Nano's back.

Landing on her feet she saw the Nano do a quick turn to face her. Laura started to back up toward the rock crevice. When her heal connected with an exposed tree root she fell, landing on her back. She then tried pushing with her feet and hands as the Nano closed in. She could only figure the animal had to be running on adrenaline now. Jaws loomed above her dripping saliva and blood. She closed her eyes.

Feeling the sudden warmth of the sun covering her eyes she opened them. Blinking she looked for the Nano. She exhaled, not realizing she had been holding her breath when she saw him lying near her, still and not moving. Laura pushed herself away and got to her feet as she watched the Nano for signs of life. Satisfied she quickly walked over to the mother raptor.

While Laura stood up to walk toward the Raptor the video on the website Ramon watched dimmed. A minute later the victor was declared as the Raptor with human pair, since one of the two were still standing. Ramon did not pay much attention to the next pair of dinosaurs to fight, an Edmarka Rex and Megalosaurus, or even the time to start because his mind was trying to comprehend what his eyes had seen. It was Mrs. Sinclair and that meant the videos were real. He quickly left his room to find his mom.

For Laura her world was very dim right now as she bent down to examine the Raptor. The Nano knew exactly how to bite and where to bite. No bones were crushed but the teeth sliced just the same. The mother raptor was conscious but loosing blood. She needed medical help. Rushing to the rock crevice she retrieved her backpack and returned to the Raptor. She had the foresight to bring some medical supplies along, praying that it was enough. She quickly set to work to stem the flow of blood. The mother raptor lay quiet, watching the two-legger. Laura had just finished when a familiar sound reached her ears. Her blood chilled, causing her to mumble, "Raptors!"

Laura looked to the forests edge. Coming toward them was a hunting pack of five. How foolish she had been, sitting out in the open. Add to that, being close to a kill that was bound to attract attention. Now they were both likely to pay for her mistake. If that were so she would not leave without a fight. Grabbing the knife she positioned herself between the five who approached and the mother raptor.

Four of the raptors quickly set on the Nano. The fifth approached Laura, quite confident in her mission. Laura could see by the way the Raptor moved with the pack that this was an alpha female. She hoped this alpha female's curiosity out-weighed her authoritive instincts.

Right now Laura was correct. The alpha female was curious. She and her pack had watched the fight from the beginning. She knew this strange Raptor could have run, but instead chose to stay and protect a two-legger. The Nano would not have been able to maintain its long, fast cheetah like stride once in the trees so the strange Raptor could have easily outrun it. Now the roles were switched as the two-legger was defending the stranger.

Several things became evident as she approached. First was the realization that the strange Raptor was also an alpha female. Second was the two-legger. She had seen the end result of the two-legger's claw, which was pointed in her direction. Then there was the two-legger's defiant stance, sending her the distinct message that this two-legger meant business and was not about to back down.

Even so she could not have this strange Raptor inside her territorial boundaries, no matter that she was just like them. Because they both competed for the same food source there was no tolerance for another predator living in their same environment, especially one that could easily be dealt with. First she had to get past the two-legger.

Laura followed the alpha as she circled them while trying to keep an eye on the others as they fed. The mother raptor lay still, not wanting to antagonize the other alpha, sensing the immediate danger they were in. When the alpha hissed loudly at her Laura knew the animal's time for being curious was over. A movement from her peripheral vision told her one of the other raptors was walking toward them. Possibly to set up an ambush or alerted by the alpha's aggressive gesture. Laura moved to keep them both in view. She tried with all her might to keep the fear at bay, knowing that her heart was beating so loud she was sure the animals could hear it. Then she realized it wasn't just her heart she heard as the wind began to blow mercilessly. All five raptors looked above her while making short alarm calls. In short time they ran as the wind and noise was too much for them.

Laura looked up as best she could while shielding her eyes. Now the *whomp, whomp, whomp* of the chopper's rotors superseded her heart. When the cage was placed nearby Laura coaxed the mother raptor inside, and then she also climbed in. Once both were secure the gate closed and the cage lifted into the air.

In less than an hour Laura and the mother raptor were back on Isle Ebony. Once they had landed Laura was allowed to exit the cage but she insisted riding along side after the cage was loaded onto the back of a truck. When both entered the lobby things changed. Maintenance men wheeled the cage toward a doorway on the opposite wall from the entrance as Mr. Davis approached Laura. She insisted on accompanying them but Mr. Davis would not hear any of it. He assured her that the Raptor would be cared for and she could check on her later. Until then it was suggested she get some rest. Laura did not want to agree but he was right. She suddenly felt very tired. She also wanted to see her husband but before she could state that fact Davis turned toward another door, motioning for her to follow. She did so reluctantly, exhaustion winning the battle. Once Laura walked through the door she was met with a set of steps leading down. At the bottom she passed through another door and into a room designed for living.

Plush carpet greeted her feet as she took in the contents of the room. A plush couch and chairs were placed strategically around another ebony fireplace. In their center was a glossy sheen, dark brown coffee table. A chandelier spread its light throughout the room since there were no windows. A few scenic pictures lined the walls and several soft sculptures were placed sporadically in the room. Even though the fireplace was not lit the room lent a comfortable atmosphere to the living space.

"You are welcome to rest here or you may choose the spare bedroom if you take the hallway to your left," related Davis.

Laura looked at the couch deciding it would do. Once she was comfortable Davis left the room. A few moments later Laura was fast asleep.

* * * * *

"Madre De Dios!" exclaimed Rosa as she watched the video Ramon had saved on his personal computer. She would not have believed that the person fighting a dinosaur was Mrs. Sinclair unless she saw it with her own eyes. Even with the proof she found it hard to believe. After the video finished Rosa went straight to the phone and dialed the police. They immediately connected her with the two officers investigating the case, Garrett and McKenzie. Rosa quickly filled them in concerning the video. Since Garrett was the one who picked up the phone he made arrangements to come over right away. When they arrived Rosa escorted them to Ramon's room. The boy sat on the side of the bed after starting the show again to give them plenty of room to watch. Once done Ramon showed them the web site.

"This is obviously a type of gambling ring and it seems they are using dinosaur fights in place of dog fights. How long have you been watching these fights?" Garrett asked.

"I have only watched two of them. I only found the site a couple of days ago. I thought they were not real until I saw Mrs. Sinclair. My mother and I both know Mrs. Sinclair very well and she would not be there of her own initiative. Something is very wrong."

"I know she is trying to find her husband," interrupted Rosa. "She loves that man very much and I know she would not leave her home and her new born son for any other reason."

McKenzie, who had been quiet for the duration took in the facial expressions of both Ramon and Mrs. Chavez. She could sense they were being honest with them. If there was one thing Tessa had on the job it was a good judge of character. Now if she could just apply it in her personal life.

After hearing his mother speak Ramon thought of something that might help. "While we waited for you to get here I noticed they have another fight scheduled for tomorrow afternoon. Maybe it will give us a clue as to where Mr. and Mrs. Sinclair are?"

"That is a possibility. What time did they schedule it for?" questioned McKenzie as she looked at the website. "Lets see, yes it looks like this one is to begin at four tomorrow afternoon."

Garrett looked at his watch. "It is just a little before five now. That gives us plenty of time to check into things."

"Yes, one thing is for sure, the fight took place on one of the islands. We just have to figure out which one. Since both are close to Costa Rica we need to contact the government and have them check out the islands."

Garrett nodded in agreement. Shortly afterwards they left with the web address and its password. Before they left they instructed Ramon to watch the fight as well in case he would see something that would click. Then they reassured him they would be in touch.

* * * * *

Laura stretched as she began to wake up. Suddenly remembering where she was she sat bolt upright. Taking in her surroundings she noted that she was alone. Her shoulders slouched a bit in relief but tensed again when she saw a round dome covering sitting on top of a hot plate. Lifting the lid the tantalizing aroma of food drifted her way. Her system responded in anticipation.

As she ate Laura wondered how long she had slept. She could not tell if it were day or night. While sitting she saw a hall leading to another area of the house. Quickly finishing her meal she got up to investigate as she was in need of the lady's room. When she walked to the end of the room she saw another hall directly opposite. Now she had a choice. Given her time span she chose the right since she remembered Davis saying a bedroom was to the left and hit pay dirt.

Shortly entering the hall she took the first door on the left, entering the bath room. She did what was needed then set about taking a quick half bath. She wanted to find her husband and check on the Raptor so twenty minutes later she exited the bathroom to do just that.

Upon entering the living room Laura stopped when she saw J.T. sitting in one of the soft chairs. She tensed, ready to do battle.

"I see that you found the bathroom."

Laura did not reply.

"You were very impressive out there Laura. The way you and the Raptor worked together. I really could use you on our team here. Maybe given time you would reconsider."

Laura was puzzled, ignoring his last comment. How could he have seen her?

"Yes, I can tell you are quite puzzled. I guess the best way to explain is to take you on a tour. Afterward you can see your husband."

As he spoke J.T. got up, walked over to a door leading to the stairway, holding it open for her. At first she balked but quickly thought better of it. Traveling up the stairs they both entered the lobby. Laura was surprised to note the sun was half way up in the sky. That meant she had slept through the evening, night, and into mid morning.

There were two other doors exiting the lobby besides the main entrance. J.T. walked toward the one on the left, opening it for her to enter. Once inside Laura was greeted with an awesome scene. At least ten to twelve people were sitting at computers while two others monitored a set of controls connected to small satellites. She had no idea that there were other people here. Beyond that was a breathtaking view. Forgetting everything and everyone in the room she walked over to the window, which extended from floor to ceiling and running the full length of the room. Her view swept over the low-lying hills and flat plains, containing small patches of water, intently watching the animals that covered them. A pair of Diplodocus waded through the water on four sturdy legs. Their long whip-like tails relaxed behind them as their long necks reached up in an arch while they watched their surroundings. Although they were slow their movements were graceful for an animal as long as a tennis court and weighing ten tons.

Large herds of Hadrosaurs dotted the landscape, each characterized by their thick, squat torsos and massive, inflexible tails. Some of them had crests on the tops of their heads, while others did not. As Laura watched she noted some occasionally walked on their four legs while others walked on their two hind legs, using their big strong tails to balance themselves. The Hadrosaurs were as numerous in their day as the Wildebeest for our day. Right now the Hadrosaurs were living up to their past.

Intermixed with them were small herds of Triceratops, Pentaceratops, and Stegosaurus. Two other large dinosaurs competed with the Diplodocus for space. The Brachiosaurus with its amazing long neck, feeding off the high tops of the trees where the Diplodocus could not lift his head as high, settling for low-growing plants, bushes and ferns. The second large dinosaur was the Titanosaurus, ranging in length from sixty to ninety feet long and weighing as much as a hundred tons. The island was immense, land extending beyond the eye could see.

Without realizing it Laura mumbled, "How?"

"That little fat man wasn't the only one bribed for specimens. There were a few of the miners who dug up the mosquitoes for the DNA who readily accepted bribes. I was able to gain quite a few specimens."

Laura felt that something was wrong. The animals did not act anxious or skittish. None of them were taking note of possible danger. Although the scene was beautiful it was also too peaceful.

"Where are the Theropods?"

"Right now, they are underground, until a scheduled fight."

Laura looked at him, not understanding.

"Again, I have caused you to be confused. Please let me show you what I mean."

Once again Laura followed J.T. Using the computers, he showed her the underground setup where the Theropods were kept and why. As he did those who worked in the room quietly moved out of the way. The moment he finished Laura was momentarily speechless, but not for long.

"So, what you are doing is a glorified scenario of dog fighting only you are using dinosaurs?"

"Yes, it is a very lucrative business. The first test run was the Spinosaurus and the T-Rex. I had my men place the Spino on the island as a young adult, watching as it grew to adulthood. When the two animals finally met it was awesome. We were fortunate to get it recorded off the satellite feed. Once it was taped a time was set for it to be viewed with bets placed. It was too bad the Spino died a few months after that, a freak accident. Got to close to a cliff as it tried to grab a plant eater."

"I remember now, during a press conference after the paleontologist's return from helping a boy get off the second island, he mentioned the Spinosaurus. He blamed it on InGenics or something, but it was you."

"Yes, the fact that there were people there bothered me at first. After a while I changed my mind because it gave me another idea."

Laura had been looking at one of the computer monitors when the full import of his words hit her, combined with remembering the frustration while trying to find the bag she whirled, facing J.T., shock evident in her eyes. "It was all a lie, a setup to get me on that island. There never was a container!"

"Yes and no. I did maneuver things so you would be on the other island, but there is a container. The reason I know this is because I already have it. The container was very easy to find. The fat idiot was such an oaf, so I had a backup plan to enforce in case the container was not delivered. A transmitter was placed inside. This allowed my men to track it easily. They were in and off the island in no time, with only one casualty, just a low order of importance on my end since I achieved my goal. Of course, I did not report it to Biosyntech because I had other plans for it. The company never knew there was a transmitter placed inside the container so to them it was a total loss."

Waving his arm in a circle over the computer room he continued, "Even though I had been an employer of Biosyntech at the time I had been working on the side with my own system while Biosyntech negotiated the theft of the fertilized eggs. I needed this container since the stupid miners gave me a bunch of plant eaters.

What I needed were the Theropods. I also apologize for using you this way but I needed to test a theory and it paid off well. The fight made me a small fortune, more than two of the other fights put together. Now let's finish the tour so you can see your husband."

At first Laura was too angry, not wanting to move. She suddenly felt as though she had walked into the lion's den, with the door slamming shut behind her. The mention of her husband was the deciding factor, making her follow J.T. to another room.

* * * * *

Ramon woke to the sound of an angry squirrel's chattering and another school morning although this one was slightly different. Most Monday mornings found him in study hall since he did not have a morning class scheduled. He liked it that way so if he wanted to sleep in he could. The only class he had was at one P.M. and it would be over in plenty of time to see the fight.

Deciding he needed to get some chores done he rousted himself from bed. His mother was working now so most of the household chores were left up to him. By eleven he was close to being done, which centered on folding a load of clothes when they finished drying. While he waited Ramon decided to do some surfing on the net. First, he checked the Clashing Dinosaurs website. The first thing he noted was the steady climb of the bidding. So far the odds favored the Edmarka Rex. While dwelling on this possibility he jumped when his land phone sounded off its ring. Quickly recovering he reached for the receiver.

"Hello?"

"Ramon Chavez?"

"Yes."

"This is Officer Rick Garrett."

Ramon remained silent, allowing the officer to speak.

"I know I told you to watch that fight this afternoon, well I need you to record it as well. Can you do that?"

"Sure, no problem."

"My shift ends right at four, when the fight starts but I will need to check in first before I take off. I will be over as soon as I finish. McKenzie contacted the Costa Rican government and they are going to check out both islands for any sign of the Sinclairs, or anyone else for that matter. See you then."

Ramon hung the receiver back onto the phone's cradle.

* * * * *

When the mother raptor first woke up she was a bit disoriented as to her surroundings due to the sleep inducing drug she had been given. The first thing she sensed was the warmth of the room combined with some strange smells and one very familiar scent, that of her own kind. This prompted her to try standing. At first she was a bit shaky while ignoring the slight pain in her side, but she managed it. As she did another scent reached her. This caused her immediate attention. Once up she searched the room for its source, now totally oblivious of the increasing pain in her side.

In a huge cage across from her were four other raptors, three males and a small female. Shifting her sight to a cage flush with her own she found what she was looking for, her alpha male. She noted he was asleep so she called to him. At first he did not answer so she called again. When he lifted his head and saw her, the mother raptor made soft clicking noises. He rose and walked toward her. Touching noses and rubbing through the bars they greeted each other, both unaware of the eyes watching them.

* * * * *

J.T. watched the small reunion. "You did an excellent job of patching her up. Our vet was quite impressed with your work. Your quick action saved the Raptor. She definitely would have bled to death if you had not stopped the bleeding. Instead of using her for research I can now use her for breeding."

After Laura walked into what J.T. referred to as the hatchery she was busy taking in the contents of the room when she heard

J.T. speak. Following his gaze she saw the two raptors. Laura walked over to the cage, which was the equivalent of a gorilla cage extending from floor to ceiling. She watched the raptors, noting the female's wounds and the fresh set of stitches spreading out in a ribbon effect. Laura was satisfied that the Raptor was going to be okay. So intent was she in examining the Raptor Laura jumped at the sudden loud crash against the bars and the loud screech coming from the alpha male. Laura sprang back from the male's cage. The mother raptor was momentarily stunned as she watched the alpha male make another lunge at Laura. Laura was also shocked as she moved more toward the female's side.

"I am sorry about that," stated J.T. Talking into a two way radio he hissed, "Davis get in here now!"

Laura looked at the alpha male, trying to comprehend the animal's actions while the mother raptor tried to calm her mate. When Davis suddenly appeared in front of the cage Laura blinked to grasp he was standing there. Both raptors recognized him immediately, hissing and showing their teeth. Davis raised the dart gun, aiming at the alpha male.

"No wait," cried Laura as the gun released the dart, finding its mark. "Why?"

"Again, my apologies Laura, they tend to get that way when they have not fed for awhile." J.T. walked up to Laura, attempting to take her by the elbow to guide her away. She would have none of it, jerking her arm from his grasp.

"What do you mean? You starve them? No wonder he tried to attack me." It was then Laura noted the men attempting to move a now sedated Raptor. "Where are you taking him?"

"It is time for the Raptor to go to his underground pen. He is due to fight in half an hour. We not only have live fights where people may attend per my discretion but we also tape record some for future playing. My staff usually leaves to go home between four or five pm. By taping the fights allows me to show them without the needed presence of my staff. I also have the animal chosen to fight taken away from their food source for a day or two, makes them feistier."

Before she could reply J.T. took Laura's elbow, a bit more forceful than before. This resulted in the mother raptor charging at J.T. Now without her mate once again she saw another of her pack in jeopardy.

"Davis," J.T. called over his shoulder. "It seems the female is feeling quite a bit better. See that she is moved back to her cage."

"No problem."

"I think we can forego the rest of the tour now. It is time to see your husband." With that spoken he guided Laura back the way they had come. The only difference, instead of going through the door to the lobby they entered one straight across the computer and satellite room. Above the door was a sign saying 'Observation Room.'

Once inside Laura quickly took in her surroundings. Her first impression was of a theater, complete with the big screen having its curtain drawn and three rows of seats. There was another door to her right with another sign reading 'To the Lobby.' To her left she was surprised to see a long cage starting five feet from where she stood to end flush with the wall. J.T. remained quiet as the contents of the cage became evident to Laura.

Seeing the man lying on the cot startled her at first but when Laura saw Bradley nothing held her back. She ran over to the cage door calling to him. At first he did not respond but with the second call he was up in a flash reaching for his wife. They tried to hold each other the best they could with the bars between them when the door suddenly opened, granting Laura access. Once she entered the door closed again but she did not care. Her world was complete now as she held the man she loved with all her heart close to her.

J.T. watched the couple for a moment longer before he turned and walked back through the door. As he worked to prepare for the fight his thoughts returned to Laura. He could now understand why his brother had been so infatuated with her. In the short time he knew her J.T. could see she was a fighter and one who was not weak minded but could make her own sound decisions. She was a person whose personality gives a guy a challenge. This complimented her feminine side allowing her movements to define her grace and confidence, enhancing her physical appearance. Because of this he so enjoyed her company. He felt with time he could almost forgive her for killing his brother...almost.

* * * * *

The minutes ticked by fast for Laura as she sat beside her husband on the cot. She explained the events that led her to him, understanding his shock and anger when she expounded further about J.T. When she was almost finished they were briefly interrupted by maintenance workers bringing the mother raptor into the room, placing her in the cage next to theirs. When Laura voiced her concern they reassured her that the Raptor would be awake shortly.

After they left Laura and Bradley sat in silence. True to their word the mother raptor woke up, a bit disoriented but all right. They jumped when the silence was broken as J.T. and Davis came into the room sitting in the back row of seats. The mother raptor responded to their appearance with a snarl and eyes narrowing slightly. A moment later the lights dimmed and the curtain pulled away to reveal an open area of land. The Nano's sudden appearance caused Laura to jump and the mother raptor to hiss.

Senses on high alert the Nano moved closer to the edge of the trees, oblivious to those who watched him. When the alpha male appeared the mother raptor's hiss changed to an alarm call, a high pitched sound that reached the male Raptor causing him to sense danger. With that came the awareness of movement behind him. He turned in time to see a gigantic head come at him to smash into his left shoulder, almost knocking him off his feet. He rebounded quickly, facing his opponent, hissing loudly and flexing his sharp claws, telling the Nano a distinct statement, the Raptor was on the defense and not backing down.

Circling the Nano looked for an opening. Jaws snapping he snarled and roared, flashing his serrated teeth. Without warning he charged forward to swing his head, knocking the Raptor to the side. The alpha male quickly recovered. His screeching roar filled the air, stressing a challenging defense against the Nano. Stomping his feet the Nano lunged in a mock charge, fell back, repeating it again. The alpha male had had enough and charged forward. Anticipating the move the Nano quickly side-stepped but not fast enough. The male Raptor sank his teeth into the Nano's leg causing the Nano to roar in pain and rage. As the Raptor brought his clawed foot up to connect with the Nano's soft underbelly the Nano bent down, clamping his jaws over the back of the Raptor's neck, pressing down with half a ton of pressure, slicing through flesh while crushing neck and vertebrae. The alpha male went limp, crumbling to the ground as Laura cried, "NO" several times, the mother raptor stared in silence and the Nano roared its victory.

* * * * *

Several hours later Officer Rick Garrett arrived at the Central division, thirty minutes before the end of his shift. He noted that other officers were doing the same, of which Tessa McKenzie was one. As he unloaded his car he waved to her. She nodded in acknowledgement. They both knew where they were headed for after they finished checking out for their shift.

After submitting their reports electronically, turning in a number of tickets, and summarizing one robbery to be put in the lineup book for the next shift they waited for the go ahead by the sergeant. Once everyone was accounted for they could leave. Twenty minutes later they were climbing into Rick's dark blue Hyundai Sonata. From there they headed down the parking ramp from the upper level, approached the gate on the North east side, and once Garrett used his pass card they were headed in the direction of the Chavez home.

They were both quiet for a bit. Tessa glanced at Rick's profile briefly, noting the set, determined look to his jaw. His gaze stayed focused on the road, a slight frown creasing his brow. She had worked with him on a few shifts so she was quite familiar with his mood and posture he was portraying, knowing that very little would move him away from the choices he made now. Still she felt she should say something. "Don't you feel that we should have turned this case over to the detectives? They are the ones that are suppose to do the follow ups."

"No, not this time. For some reason I feel that we would be better suited for helping the Sinclair's."

"I see. So it is just a case of your 'man's intuition'?"

As she smiled Rick gave her a quick side-ways look. "Call it gut instinct," he stated.

Tessa shook her head, still smiling as Rick parked the car in front of the Chavez home. Opening their respective doors to exit the car both stopped when Rick's cell phone started playing an indistinct musical melody. Quickly snatching it he answered without thinking, "Officer Rick Garrett speaking. How may I help you?" He silently chided himself for answering his personal phone in his professional voice. He was quiet for a moment.

"Yes…Bernard Sanchez. Good to hear from you." Rick looked over at Tessa and she understood.

"What did you find out…Yes…Okay, thank you?"

Hanging up he looked at Tessa. "Sanchez said they did a complete search of both islands short of not physically going onto each one. They used helicopters and ships, scouring the whole area, finding nothing but a fishing boat passing by and a lot of dinosaurs."

"So where could she be?"

"I don't know."

"She has to be in an area where there are dinosaurs and those are the only two islands containing them. Not to mention the fact that someone is using dinosaurs, pitting them against each other. That means there are other people involved, most likely the ones who kidnapped Mr. Sinclair and now Mrs. Sinclair as well."

As Tessa spoke Rick's mind was moving fast, putting things together in his mind, the website, the fights, and the disappearance of two people with one showing up on a video on that same website, and the non human habitation of both islands. "Then there may be another island somewhere, Tessa. Let's go look at that video."

* * * * *

Laura and Bradley sat in silence on their cot, still surrounded by the bars that encased them. The mother raptor, after seeing her mate killed lay quietly in her nest. Laura worried about her but there was nothing she could do. While she relished the comfort of her husband's arms she could feel the raptors loneliness. She knew that J.T. had to be stopped, but how.

The minutes ticked by slowly, even though it had been only an hour since the fight when J.T. appeared before them once again. His abrupt departure right after the fight went unnoticed by the three contained in the cage. Now, as he stood in front of the couple they looked at him with loathing and contempt while the Raptor lay quietly watching. Noting the Raptor's lackadaisical manner J.T. did not say anything and soon left the room. Two minutes later Davis entered to tranquilize the mother raptor. Laura could do nothing but watch in silence as they moved the Raptor. Bradley, on the other hand had other ideas. "Where are you taking her now? Haven't you done enough damage?"

Keeping one eye on the maintenance men as they moved the Raptor Davis, for some reason decided to answer Bradley, "We are moving her to a cage near the other raptors in the hope that her depression will lighten up. J.T. wants her for breeding so he wants to keep her happy as much as possible."

"Then you should not have killed the alpha male, her mate," snapped Laura.

Davis ignored her as he followed the maintenance men out of the room. The sound of the door closing echoed through the sudden silence filling the room, but only for a short while.

* * * * *

Ramon sat at his computer while Rick and Tessa stood on each side of him. On the monitor the video ran showing two major predators fighting a bloody battle. A Megalosaurus, weighing in at one ton, thirty feet long and ten feet in height flexed its powerfully hinged jaws and flashed its curved, serrated teeth while lashing out with sharp talloned claws a number of times in an attempt to win. The Edmarka Rex, being of the same family as the Megalosaurus was slightly larger than his opponent, thirty-five feet long, two tons, and fourteen feet tall he inflicted wounds in counter measure to the Megalosaurus. Even though he was larger the battle did not go his way as it soon turned toward the Megalosaurus. His wounds were numerous but he did not mind as he bent down to feed and the video dimmed. Little was known about this dinosaur but one thing was proven solid, he was one ferocious and determined animal.

For a while no one in the room spoke. Both officers stared at the monitor at first stunned, then puzzled. Rick was the first to speak, "Did you see what I saw?"

Tessa nodded her head.

"Ramon, can you show both videos at the same time, the one with Laura Sinclair and this one?"

"Yes I can."

Ramon quickly started both videos, a bit smaller view but it was enough.

"There," Rick snapped. "Pause the first one… now the second. Look do you see it? Ramon did you tape the very first fight?"

"No, but I can tell you it is like the one we just watched."

Tessa saw it the same time Rick did, "The landscape, they are different. The one with Laura Sinclair does not match the other two. The land has more brush, debris, rock formations whereas the land in the videos with just the dinosaurs look as though the grass has been cut with a lawnmower while the trees are positioned in such a way as to form an outside wall with a small entrance in the center. Almost like a stage."

"Exactly, there is no way a setup like this could be on one of the two islands. The helicopters would have seen it right away."

"Then there has to be another island, but where?"

Ramon watched the two as they conversed but when they mentioned the prospect of another island his first response was, "What, a third island, but where?"

"Good question," Rick quipped. How many islands are there in the tropics?"

"I did a school report last year on tropical islands and there are several dozen islands in Costa Rica. Then there are ones uncharted."

Tessa sighed, "So we can leave out the idea of the Costa Rican government searching the islands for us."

"We have two goals here," Rick stressed. "Which is to get the Sinclair's off the island safely and shut down this business. Right now we are stumped as to the location of the island so we need to find a way to shut them down."

Rick moved to walk about the room as his mind tried to come up with a solution. As he did his eyes fell on all the computer equipment in the room? "You a computer wiz kid of some kind?"

Ramon hesitated a moment wondering where this line of questioning was going and if he may be in some kind of trouble. "The word you are looking for is hacker."

"Yes of course. If I remember correctly a hacker can easily go into a system and cause it harm."

"Yes they can, but if you are referring to me, I am not a malicious hacker."

"But...you...can, if you wanted too."

Ramon thought for a moment. "You want to know if I can get into this gambling web site's computer networking system and shut it down."

Rick nodded his head while saying, "Yes."

Ramon smiled as he understood where Garrett was going. "That would be no problem officer."

"Great, now all we have to do is figure out where the island is so we can get the Sinclair's off first. Did the site announce when the next fight was to take place?"

"Just that it was a special fight scheduled for late Saturday morning. They are being quite mysterious as to what dinosaurs are fighting, an SR and HM. Bidding is the same."

"Why the initials?" queried Tessa. What is so special about that?"

"It could be just to add to the mystery of the fight?"

At Ramon's sudden intake of breath both officers looked at him, puzzled. "Special, the word special, I know how you can find the island!" With that Ramon turned back to the computer and brought up the web site. Both officers came to look over his shoulder, curious. "There is a link." Scrolling down the web page a bit Ramon found it. "Yes, there it is, a link called 'Special Guests'. Ramon clicked on the link bringing up the form for attending a live fight. Both officers looked at the form in disbelief.

Tessa was the first to speak. "Is this for real?"

"The fights are real enough so yes, I believe so."

Still looking at the form Rick's mind began to form a plan. A moment later he stepped back, looking at Tessa. Their eyes met. "Well Mrs. Rick Garrett, I think we deserve to spend our second wedding anniversary on a tropical island."

Tessa smiled, understanding completely while at the same time ignoring the light fluttering of her heart. Even though she is a police officer for the central division in San Diego she was still a woman in mind and body. The fact she had feelings for Rick were inconsequential at this time, especially since she was just recovering from a bad relationship with a married man. How was she to know he was married?

For the next hour the three spent the time filling in the application. When they got to the part about the fee they were stumped since the amount was a lot.

"Well now what do we do?" Tessa felt truly at a loss. "There is no way we can ask for that amount from the department, especially without an explanation."

Ramon solved the problem easily by volunteering the use of his job savings. At first both officers vehemently objected until Ramon threatened to go on his own and that he did not mind if it brought the Sinclair's home safely.

"Think of it this way," he reasoned further, "Since you will be using my debit card, your teenage son just brought you a surprise anniversary gift."

Rick nodded his approval at the boy's cleverness. "This means we will have to use Ramon's last name. Thanks kid, we owe you big time and we will pay your money back."

"Thanks but my pay back will be the safe return of Laura and Bradley."

Once the payment was made and acknowledged a message was sent to Ramon's email account. Opening it they received their instructions of which consisted of being ready to leave by ten p.m. Friday night and a car would be there to escort them to the airport.

From the information Tessa proposed a theory, "I think it would be a good idea to contact the airport and put the bug in their ear to watch for any suspicious planes wanting to gain permission to land and to notify us right away."

"Good idea. I also think we need to form a strategy plan of sorts. We don't know what the situation is on that island before we can devise a good escape route. Ramon, you will, of course stay here to man the computers. Once we are safely off I will call you to let you know the coast is clear to shut the system down."

"If there is some kind of emergency we need some kind of communication," Tessa reasoned.

"Well you already have cell phones in order to call me," declared Ramon "Just send me a text."

Rick nodded his head in agreement. "Great idea, we have four days to get ready so let's get busy."

After exchanging phone numbers and realizing Rick would need to upgrade his phone both officers left leaving Ramon to start his side of things. Since it was only mid evening he decided to start right away. Moving over just a bit he logged into another PC that he liked to use for those special hacking jobs, one he could monitor closely while working on other things. Since he had gained access to one of the servers Ramon decided to install a rootkit.

He was excited about this new venture because it would give him the chance to use his newly developed rootkit. This meant that the rootkit had to be built before he could install it into a computer system. This he did by assembling and saving the tools required for rootkit development. The rootkit toolkit had taken a lot of time but it was necessary as it allowed him to research, develop, design and package his rootkit without any distractions. Three important tools were a big help to him, which included a Driver Development Kit (DDK), a Software Development Kit (SDK), and a C compiler.

Another tool he included was the Debugging Tools for Windows and the symbols needed in order for the tool to work. By the time his toolkit was complete it contained twelve items. The final thing he did before he started to develop his rootkit was to zip and archive the components. His collection was something he could take pride in for years to come.

Now, with his collection of tools and a newly developed rootkit he could use it to hide his presence on the computer system used on the island while gathering data. This meant he could interact with network resources, files and other systems, and once he gained administrative rights he would be able to do things with the network, basically running free. Once he was inside some of his tools in the rootkit would work to keep him hidden by cleaning log files and erasing evidence of the intrusion. It was imperative that he evade detection by firewall software, antivirus software, or any other security applications.

Since most rootkits were designed to load during the boot process Ramon decided to use "demand start" loading, which allowed him to load his rootkit whenever he wanted. To begin he built the loader by entering the code then compiled the program. From there he created a configuration file by opening a DOS Command Prompt window. He then moved the rootkit to c:\comint32.sys directory and started the rootkit with the command "net start MyDeviceDriver." When he saw the words 'Driver Loaded' he knew his rootkit was loaded and running. At this point his rootkit could only hide its configuration file and device driver entry from the operating system. There were many more things to add if he were to achieve true stealth. He spent the rest of the night working on the rootkits other additions. He was barely aware of the time or when his mom checked on him.

❋ ❋ ❋ ❋ ❋

Metriacanthosaurus paced in his fifty by fifty foot pen, anxiety evident in his features. He glanced overhead at the bright glowing object suspended a hundred feet above his head. He snarled, perplexed because he could not reach it when a sound behind him caused him to turn. At first he did not know what to make of the opening but when other sounds and smells reached him he passed through to find himself in a long tunnel.

For the moment he was confused but the smell of fresh air touching his nostrils changed his mind. Turning to the right he followed the scent. A moment later he burst through the opening, entering the arena. The brightness of the sun momentarily blinded him causing him to roar in frustration and anger. Recovering quickly he allowed the warmth of the sun to penetrate his body as he took his first tentative steps into the open.

At first glance one would think he looked like a t-rex, although the spine, running from the back of his neck, across the back, ending at the middle of its tail, gave one the image of a Spinosaurus. Stretching forward as he walked the spine gave him a distinctive hump-backed appearance. Stopping for a moment he raised his head, showing his height of eleven feet as he sniffed the air for the scent of prey. Being unsuccessful he searched his surroundings for movement. Feeling restless he roared again, alerting another dinosaur to his presence.

The Dryptosaurus had just reached the opening to the arena when he heard the roar of the Metriacanthosaurus. He immediately ceased his forward momentum. His jaw opened slightly in a mock snarl while flexing his eight-inch long finger claws. Moving forward cautiously he soon located the source of the roar. Pausing again, he contemplated his plan of attack, waiting for the right moment to ambush the Metria. His long eagle-like claws on each foot dug into the earth, preparing to propel his big muscular legs forward as the Metria moved closer. When the Metria was within striking distance and facing away from him he burst from the trees. Using his speed he reached the Metria in a few short strides. Once close enough the Dryptosaurus launched himself into the air, to land onto the back of the Metria just as the Metria turned to snap at the sudden sound from behind.

The Metria had little chance to defend itself as one point two tons of flesh and bones landed on top, snapping his back. Even so he tried to bite his attacker while bringing his feet up to slice but the Dryptosaurus worked too fast. Clamping his mouth over the neck of the Metria he sliced with his finger claws and toes, slashing and ripping flesh. The Metria quickly ceased his movements.

Inside the observation room Davis, who had been watching the fight with J.T. stood up to leave, clearly annoyed with the results. "Well that was a disappointment. Now we will have to do the fight all over again."

"Yes, you are right but I think we can still use this one. Next time we will release the Dryptosaurus first."

Laura, who was clearly sickened by the needless carnage she had just witnessed could not believe what she was hearing. "Did anyone bother to do any type of research on these animals before you decided to put them against each other? If you had you would have known that the Dryptosaurus excels in ambushing its prey and he has a unique and complex ankle design, allowing it to leap on its prey. To give the Metriacanthosaurus a fair chance, yes you should have released the Dryptosaurus first. The Metriacanthosaurus should not have been partnered with the Dryptosaurus. It was thought that he may have been a pack hunter, otherwise there is little known about him. He is one you would need to study for a while, find out how he defends himself, his hunting pattern, his fighting technique, how he gets along with those of his own kind, etc."

J.T. watched her for a moment before he responded, hoping that she would now see the need for her to stay here to work for him. "Now you can surely see one of the reasons I want you to work for us. Your knowledge and expertise would be of great value here."

"No J.T., I can never condone this type of business. These animals are not meant to live this way."

J.T.'s features changed. His jaw clenched tight, eyes squinting to mere slits as thoughts of his brother being rejected in this very same manner flashed through his mind, how he must have felt, even though he never let on, except when in J.T.'s presence. Quickly composing himself he relaxed his features. "Then maybe I could convince you by showing you the rest of the tour you missed out on. There are some things you may find quite interesting.

Now it was Bradley's turn to feel threatened. He had been sitting on the cot beside his wife while listening to the conversation and, at the same time admiring her tenacity, but when J.T. chose to suddenly separate them he wanted none of it. Something was not right. Standing up he put himself between J.T. and Laura. "No, she stays here, with me."

Instead of getting angry J.T. just looked at him, arching a brow. "Such theatrics are not necessary, Mr. Sinclair. I have no intention of harming Laura." Even though his thoughts desired to teach her a lesson he ignored them for now.

Laura walked up to her husband to reassure him. Touching his arm she got his attention. "Bradley, I will be okay. I won't be gone long."

"I don't like it. Why doesn't he just let us go?"

"Good question. I wish I knew."

Davis walked over to open a small door built into the frame of the cage, allowing Laura to pass through. Meeting J.T. at the door to the computer lab J.T. held the door for her to pass through then, looking at Davis he nodded once and followed Laura.

Vince Davis understood what needed to be done. Leaving the room for a brief time he returned with a small wagon. Approaching the cage he stood facing Bradley. Before Bradley could react Davis removed the dart pistol he always carried with him, aimed it at Bradley, and fired. Bradley's reaction was immediate. He lunged at Davis, trying to reach him through the bars. Davis stood his ground, standing just beyond Bradley's grasp. His face remained impassive as he watched Bradley succumb to the drug.

* * * * *

After spending the day in school Ramon sat at his computer watching his monitor as the Dryptosaurus shot out of his hiding spot to land on a dinosaur he was not familiar with. His rootkit proved more than he had hoped for. As Ramon progressed further into the network he could actually look through the video feed, since the computers controlled them.

After the fight he moved to another camera which revealed a long corridor. A few men wearing clothes resembling a maintenance uniform walked up and down the passageway pulling a wagon hauling chunks of meat. As they traveled each would stop periodically to drop off several chunks into slots built into the walls. Intermixed were some workers pushing wheelbarrows or pulling wagons containing shovels, rakes and other tools.

Seeing enough Ramon chose another camera, noting this one had a label attached, Allosaurus. Switching over Ramon found he was looking down into a containment room. He watched an Allosaurus feasting on a pile of meat. The room was huge, made of pressed, reinforced steal.

Switching again he watched a Spinosaurus pace back and forth in its large room. Ramon was awestruck. The animal was at least sixty feet in length. Its skull was long, like a crocodile. The teeth were conical in shape and with enough spacing to allow for grabbing, puncturing and gripping its prey. The two massive arms were longer than a man. Ramon guessed at least seven feet. There were three huge claws on each arm, at least a good fifteen inches curving up. They reminded Ramon of industrial meat hooks. Elongated spines jutted straight up from the back forming a beautiful sail. As the Spino turned in his pacing Ramon took note of the immense legs, reinforced hips and flexible feet. This animal was meant to run. Being cooped up in the room was not good.

Ramon decided to look in on the other dinosaurs later and switched to a different camera titled Hatchery. He was greeted by the immediate presence of a large room with huge incubators, small pens and huge cages. His immediate attention was drawn to the two occupants standing in the center of the room. At first he could not believe it but, yes he had found Laura Sinclair. Taking note that she was not alone he was puzzled as to the person she was with for the man was not her husband. They were also in an intense conversation. The anger in the man's eyes, facial expression, and rigid stance was clearly evident. Laura remained clam but determined, shaking her head negatively while her body language revealed a defensive stance. It was obvious her calm but defiant attitude is what enraged him, causing the man to grab Laura's arm resulting in her resistance by moving one foot back, pulling away from him. Both were momentarily distracted by the sudden charge of one of the raptors against its cage. Even though Ramon could not hear the argument he could feel the rage of the animal as it berated the enclosure in an attempt to reach the man. All the man did in response was to snarl an expletive and drag Laura from the room.

Ramon sat for a moment as he let this entire scene sink in. A short time later he was sending a text. He did not have to wait long for an answer.

Later that night, after their shift Rick and Tessa arrived at Ramon's home. He quickly informed them of what had transpired, relating the fight between the dinosaurs, the one between the man and Mrs. Sinclair, and showing them the setup; how the animals were kept and released. He then took them into the network so they could see the animals for themselves. They were appalled at the condition the dinosaurs were in. It looked as though the floor was made of a strong mesh material over half of the room, which allowed the feces to pass below, at least most of it, into a type of sewage area. Some of the animals would claw at the walls, charge, battering the interior with their bodies or pace relentlessly back and forth.

Having enough Ramon tried to locate the man who had argued with Mrs. Sinclair. He searched for over five minutes with no success. Tessa suggested he come to the Division's building to meet with their sketch artist. Ramon agreed but stated he would not be able to arrive until later that day as he had another full day of school. No one mentioned their fears of not finding Mr. Sinclair during their search for the stranger.

＊ ＊ ＊ ＊ ＊

Laura sat on the cot alone, staring past the bars enclosing her, seething inside. After J.T.'s sudden outburst in the Hatchery and her defiant refusal of his outlandish proposal he had made his intentions unquestionably clear-cut, beginning with Bradley. Her husband was to leave the island and she would never see him again, or her son. When J.T. was finished Laura was stunned. All she could do was stare at him, her eyes wide, and her mouth agape. He was totally mad if he thought she would stay here with him. She had no desire for this man. What was he thinking? Laura knew she would fight him, tooth and nail.

*****

Jim Thatcher walked into the computer room, quite pleased with himself. He was tired of holding himself back, trying to be Mr. Nice Guy. J.T. felt it was only fair for Laura to stay here, in place of his brother since she was the one responsible for his death. Also, once her husband was gone, she could please him in other ways his brother could not. In his mind this was reasonable because he had lost someone, he loved so she should also. He knew, with time she would get over it and accept the inevitable.

*****

The next couple of days sped by quickly for Ramon. Both were school days, although, after Wednesday classes he had met with the Central Division's sketch artist, and between the two of them had developed a portrait of the man Ramon had seen. Once the sketch was on its way to be identified he left. At home he explored the network some more. He discovered the controls for opening and closing the cages and looked at a few more enclosed dinosaurs. By the end of Wednesday, he had watched two more taped fights.

As Friday morning dawned, he was found sequestered at his personal computer working at programming a game. Fridays were usually spent this way for most of the day, designing video games, since his school week ended on Thursdays. Close to Friday evening he practiced his martial arts, emphasizing mental discipline, control, and relaxed awareness. He had always been interested in the martial arts since he was a child, although the raw strength and physical toughness never appealed to him. This Friday was no different since he would be done, with plenty of time to spare before the car came to pick up Rick and Tessa. By eight pm Ramon was engrossed in his favorite meditation discipline, Zen when the doorbell rang. When he opened the door, he was greeted by a delivery boy who promptly handed him an envelope and left.

*****

This time, when Bradley woke up, he found himself enclosed in a room lined with reinforced steel and a strong kind of mesh floor. The evident odor and claw marks on the wall told Bradley a dangerous animal had been kept here at one time. He had no idea as to why he was being kept here but his rage was just more equal to, if not more than the dinosaur that had preceded him.

* * * * *

At nine thirty-five everything was ready to go. Rick and Tessa sat on Ramon's front porch rereading the note that had been delivered. It turned out to be a reminder that the car would be there, promptly at ten and they only needed a small bag with one change of clothes and toiletries. The first reaction when they found out about the note was to bag it for analysis, but they quickly changed their minds when the message requested, they were to bring it with them, or they were not allowed into the car.

Rick refolded the small piece of paper, placed it back in its corresponding envelope and put it inside his coat pocket. "It would seem they are not taking any chances of being discovered."

"Yes, I agree. Did you hear anything back on that sketch yet?"

"Yes, the report came in just this afternoon. I was hoping to discuss it with you. The sketch resembles a man named Jeff Thatcher. When I checked further, I found out he was Laura Sinclair's boss."

"Was?"

"He died last year."

The conversation suddenly ceased as a shiny Mercury Marques pulled to a stop in front of the house. As Ramon watched from his bedroom the two officers entered the car, then turning around the vehicle drove back the way it had come.

* * * * *

The next morning Ramon was up early. After a quick shower he returned to his room. Donning a white tee shirt and jeans he padded on bare feet to the kitchen to wolf down his breakfast. He wasn't really hungry so he ate to please his mom. A short time later, as he entered his room he noted his mom entering the bathroom for a nice relaxing bubble bath. Saturdays were her days to unwind, spending a little time for herself.

Approaching his computers Ramon checked to make sure all was working well. Once he felt confident everything was running to his satisfaction Ramon sat down to wait. While he did, he decided to check out some of the other dinosaur rooms. His first choice was the Saurophaganax. This animal was something else, being close in size to the Spinosaurus. From checking his notes and reference material he found online he found there was little known about its behavior, a rare one indeed.

Ramon skipped the Acrocanthosaurus, having watched it fight the day before with the Spinosaurus. He knew that pen would be empty. He also noted three of the rooms held some type of Raptor, a Megaraptor, Sinraptor and the Velociraptor. Choosing the camera for the Velociraptor he was taken totally by surprise as he found instead, Bradley Sinclair looking disheveled but alive.

For a moment Ramon was puzzled as to why Mr. Sinclair was in such a room used for….Ramon's eyes grew round as cold reality set in. Quickly leaving that PC he went to the one with the website. Why hadn't he remembered to check it before now? Sure enough it had changed. He never saw the outlandish bidding as he looked to see the two opponents, both jumping at him as though alive, Human Male vs. Sinraptor.

"No!" he breathed. He had to tell Rick and Tessa fast. He quickly reached for his cell phone but was again stunned when he saw it was not in its usual resting spot. For a moment panic threatened him but he quickly gained control, thinking rationally. His mind raced through his routine from the time he used his cell last till now. Then it hit him, the bathroom, when he took his shower. He had placed it on top of the clothes hamper.

Rushing to the room he opened the door without thinking and was taken aback from the sudden scream of alarm coming from inside, causing him to close the door quickly, forgetting his mother was taking a bubble bath. He silently cursed. Now what was he to do? He could not go in until his mother finished. That was one of the strict rules of the household, not to interrupt his mom's bubble bath. So he waited, pacing back-and-fourth as the minutes ticked by, but to him seemed like hours. When the door finally opened he released an exasperated sigh, which his mother quickly picked up on as she entered the hall in her bathrobe. He ignored the steely look she gave him as he brushed past her. Walking over to the hamper he stopped short. The moment he saw his phone gone his mother's voice reached him. "If you are looking for your phone I put it in the cupboard above the hamper. Leaving it where you did was not a good place for it."

Rolling his eyes he quickly retrieved his phone from the cupboard, and then raced back to his room. Once there he closed the bedroom door. Sitting at his computer station he quickly wrote a text of what he found and what should he do, if anything. After he sent it he looked up at the website, noting the intense increase of the betting and hoping they would get the text before the fight started. They had less than half an hour.

＊ ＊ ＊ ＊ ＊

After exiting the plane Rick and Tessa, along with four others were escorted, via a small overland vehicle to the front of a very impressive building. A sign saying 'Welcome to Isle Ebony' greeted them as their guide took them through the glass doors leading into a lobby. Their guide quickly ushered them to another door, giving them very little time to study their surroundings. The sign above this door said Observation Room.

Laura sat in the front row with Davis sitting on her left and J.T. on her right when she heard the door open. She watched several people enter the room as J.T. got up to great his guests.

J.T. was pleased with the individuals he had chosen, two couples, which include a rich tycoon, Rick Chavez and his wife Tessa who, it seemed liked to live modestly, not wanting to flaunt their riches. The second couple consisted of a drug lord, gangster type individual called Lester "The Snake" Colton. It was clear he had led a hard life with his chiseled but battered face, thin straight nose, and bushy eyebrows shielding dark solemn eyes. Right now he attempted to portray a casual stance with his dark hair tied back into a short ponytail while wearing an off-white button down shirt and khakis. On his arm was his escort, a buxom brunette with an orange streak in her dark curls, wore an orange Sara Berman Crystal button flapper dress and black laced high-heeled sandals with painted orange toenails showing through. J.T. hoped that her constant smacking while chewing her gum would not bother him.

The next person in the group was a casino owner from Nevada USA called Tom Colony. He was a tall man wearing a maroon dress shirt and black trousers, which revealed some thickening at the waist. Crows feet radiated from the corners of each eye, which were close set. A broad, slightly flat nose rested on a thick brown mustache. It was obvious to J.T. that this man was a drinker.

Once Tom Colony was seated J.T. greeted his final guest who went by the name of Jeb Gorson. A medium height guy with a pinched face, ferret-like eyes, hair graying at the temples and wearing a black toupee he returned the greeting with a smile that revealed a slight overbite. Adding to the mix was his grey flannel suit and a silk blue tie. He was obliviously a hundred percent politician. Satisfied that everyone was seated comfortably J.T. took his seat beside Laura.

Laura, on the other hand did not look closely at the people who walked into the room except for two of them. The moment she saw Rick Garrett and Tessa McKenzie she was surprised, shocked, and then elated. For once she felt positive about finding a way off the island.

Rick and Tessa were also happy to have found Mrs. Sinclair so fast. Sitting behind her, in the second row they inspected their surroundings, trying to decide an appropriate time to make their move.

"Hi you two, my name is Dixie-May Summers." Rick and Tessa jumped at the sound of the voice and its pitch. They had stayed to themselves on the flight so as to watch each others back, being aware of the company traveling with them. Now, since Dixie-May was seated on the other side of Rick she decided it was time to make new friends. "Wow, I can't wait for the fight to start. I have never seen one before. It sounds so exciting."

Rick smiled, nodding his head as he looked in her direction, noting immediately the hoop earrings and bangle bracelets. "It is my first live performance too." When he felt a light touch on his left arm he turned back toward Tessa, silently grateful for the interruption.

"I almost forgot dear. Shouldn't you call our son to tell him we landed safely?" When J.T. turned slightly to look over his shoulder at her she explained, "He is such a sweet boy. He spent his monthly allowance so we could go on this trip, a surprise anniversary gift. We are celebrating twenty beautiful years together."

J.T. mumbled a quick happy anniversary, wondering what the boy's monthly salary actually was, and then turned to face the viewing window. Rick reached for his cell phone, turned it on and was immediately greeted with Ramon's text. As he read the message the curtain opened and he felt Tessa stiffen beside him before he heard her gasp, followed closely by Mrs. Sinclair's scream.

* * * * *

Bradley did not know what to think when the door to his room suddenly opened. For a moment he just stood looking at it, puzzled. Walking over to the door he peered cautiously through the opening. Half expecting someone to forcibly push him back inside he was surprised to find an empty passageway. Once he saw shafts of light he made his choice, heading in their direction. When he entered a clearing and came face to face with a building he recognized it immediately. At that moment he heard an angry roar from deep within the tunnel. He knew then that he was in deep trouble and the loud commotion behind him confirmed it.

* * * * *

Rick's head jerked up fast in reaction to the sudden tension in the room, causing several things to happen at once. The moment he saw Bradley run for the trees a ten foot high Sinraptor rushed into the open area while Laura Sinclair's words echoed through his head as she turned on J.T. "You bastard. You told me he had left the island! You lied to me!"

When Rick saw the Sinraptor move toward Bradley Rick quickly sent a text back to Ramon: "LET ANOTHER ONE LOOSE—NOW!"

Ramon jumped when his phone beeped saying he received a text. After reading it he frowned. Another what, dinosaur, Raptor? Sensing the urgency he opted for the later, releasing all the raptors.

* * * * *

The moment Bradley reached the trees he heard the cracking and snapping of branches and trees as the Sinraptor followed him. Darting quickly to the left, running parallel to the clearing he broke into full view again a few feet down from where he had first entered. Once clear of the foliage he ran full out toward the tunnel, knowing he had little time. There had to be someplace in that tunnel where he could hide or another door to get through.

Halfway there Bradley stopped dead in his tracks, his heart pumping, adrenaline rushing through him as the Sinraptor broke into the clearing behind him. Both now faced another dinosaur. It stood there thirteen feet in height, watching him. When the dinosaur caught sight of the Sinraptor the animal roared loudly and charged. Bradley turned to look at the Sinraptor. He could tell the animal was now focused on this new threat. Waiting a second more he suddenly broke straight away heading for the trees as the two animals faced each other in combat.

* * * * *

When J.T. saw the Megaraptor enter the arena he stood up, his face distorted and white with rage he shouted, "How did that animal get loose?! Davis, come with me, now!"

Once the door closed behind them Laura began to struggle with the bonds holding her hands to the chair. When she saw a small blade come close to her wrist she stiffened. Watching it turn slightly the blade sliced quickly through the strands encircling her arm. A quick repeat of her left arm and she was free.

With a quick thank you glance toward Rick she turned toward the maintenance door. Without hesitating she entered into the arena before Rick could stop her. Once the door closed behind her Laura moved straight out until she reached the clearing. Briefly glancing at the struggling dinosaurs she turned toward the forest and shouted Bradley's name several times. When she stopped yelling the air suddenly stilled. Laura looked again at the dinosaurs. The fight was over. The Megaraptor moved in to feed.

"Laura!"

When she heard her name called she did not ask from whence it came. Turning away from the feeding frenzy she ran into her husband's outstretched arms. At that precise moment the outside world did not exist as they both comforted and reassured each other before they moved away.

Catching the movement from the corner of his eye the Megaraptor paused briefly while feeding. Being very intelligent prompted him to form a sense of curiosity and the small creatures moving around by the forests edge set those feelings in motion. Quickly swallowing a chunk of meat he flexed his thirteen inch talloned claws on his forearms and moved forward to investigate.

＊ ＊ ＊ ＊ ＊

The moment Laura and Bradley entered the Observation Room they were greeted by Rick and Tessa. The others meandered nearby. Laura returned the greeting, "It is so good to see you two. Please let's leave before J.T and Davis get back here."

"My thoughts exactly, replied Rick.

"Look!"

Everyone looked at Dixie-May.

"Look at the door—the door!"

Their gaze turned to where Dixie-May pointed. Laura gasped when she saw the door's latch move up, then down and back again.

Bradley was the first to speak again, "Please don't tell me they are like your Raptor Laura."

"Okay I won't but we have to leave—now!"

A sudden loud crash from the door made them all jump and the Megaraptor's head shot through the opening as the door landed at their feet. The animal roared loudly in frustration and anger. Everyone in the room scrambled toward a door as the animal pulled back then charged through sending pieces of plaster and wood in all directions.

Rick, Tessa, and the others ran parallel with the viewing window toward the exit door leading into the lobby. Rick held the door so the others could pass through. Looking back he saw the Megaraptor gain its footing and focus on the fleeing figures of Laura and Bradley as they made their way toward the exit door to the Computer Room.

"Mrs. Sinclair, Laura!"

Reaching the door Laura glanced over at Rick, seeing him point at the Megaraptor as it ran toward them. She gasped, "Get those people to safety!" Then they were both gone, the door closing behind them. Rick did the same. As the group raced outside no one took note of the lobby door standing open as they ran through, or the complete disarray of the room as one of the group stepped on a small broken chess piece lying on the floor. Once everyone was outside Rick quickly looked for the small vehicle that brought them here. It was no where in sight.

"Rick, what happened to the small car?"

"Good question, Tessa. Our guide must have taken it. We will have to go on foot."

Several bits of cussing and groaning reached Rick's ears. He ignored them as he and Tessa walked toward the trees. The others quickly followed when they heard the Megaraptor roar from within the building. They soon disappeared in the forest.

* * * * *

J.T. sat at one of the computers trying to figure out what went wrong. He had only himself to blame for letting his crew leave shortly after the Sinraptor was released. Davis sat at another computer to try and find a reason his boss would be comfortable with. What he found was just the opposite.

"Sir, I think we should leave, right now."

J.T. looked at him as though he had lost his senses.

"The Megaraptor was not the only one released. It seems that all the raptors are loose."

J.T.'s face suddenly turned ashen. Without speaking he got up, Davis following suit. Moving toward the lobby door they stopped when the door to the observation room opened allowing Laura and Bradley to enter. Quickly closing it behind them they raced to the other entrance to the lobby. When the doorway closed behind them again J.T. had had enough. "Get her back here!"

Davis took off toward the lobby door. Halfway there the door and wall to his left exploded sending shards of plaster and splintered wood in all directions, and landing Davis on his back. Dazed at first he did not know what had happened until he felt something warm drop on his head. Looking up he barely had time to scream as the jaws of death descended.

✳ ✳ ✳ ✳ ✳

The moment the Megaraptor entered the room J.T. fell back against one of the computers while trying to shield his head from any flying debris. Recovering quickly J.T. saw the Megaraptor find Davis. Knowing he had little time he ducked behind the wall surrounding one of the two servers in the room. Through the cracks J.T. watched the dinosaur turn into a live tornado as it tried to figure out where the rest of the small creatures had gone. His search soon netted him something of more value. Locating the large scenic window he saw large herds grazing, oblivious to any danger. The Megaraptor screeched loudly, charging forward. CPUs, monitors, printers, and the other server were crushed and destroyed in the animal's path, causing the room to darken. J.T. came out of his hiding place when he heard the sound of breaking glass. What he saw sickened him. The computer room was completely destroyed resulting in total power loss because of the one server. Since that one server was connected to the one he took refuge nearby, it too was down. There was no way the servers could be brought back up and power restored in time to prevent the dinosaurs below ground from getting out. To top it off the Megaraptor now lay dead just inside the window after a big shard of glass felled the animal. Swearing profusely J.T. left the building with one goal in mind, to find Laura Sinclair and make her pay for this.

Moving carefully over the sandy clearing J.T. quickly located their tracks. Taking off in the direction they set J.T. soon disappeared into the woods. He had two distinct advantages in finding Laura, the fact that he was an excellent tracker, having hunting expeditions on the island with his brother, and the fact he knew every inch of his Isle Ebony. He only had to follow their trail a short way to know the direction they were going and how he could intercept the couple.

* * * * *

Ten minutes into the walk Rick and the others found their path blocked. Stretching before them was a huge clearing of land containing several herds of herbivores grazing peacefully. If they went around, skirting the perimeter of the grazing animals their time would be extended for reaching the helicopter. The best way would be to walk straight through. They had a good two miles to go and the faster they reached their destination the better their chances were to getting off this island in one piece. The only one not sure of their options was Jeb. "Well now what are we going to do? How are we going to get to the other side?"

Most politicians were avid talkers who loved to listen to the sound of their own voice and, for some reason Mr. Jeb Gorson had kept silent up to this point. Now of all times he had to voice his opinions. For Dixie-May there was only one option, while at the same time being excited about the prospect? "I think it would be fun and thrilling to walk with them. I mean, aren't they just like cattle?"

Tessa smiled at the woman's naivety and innocence. "That is true but they are still wild animals and should be treated with caution."

Even so we will have to walk through the herds." Tessa looked at Rick. "It would take to long for us to go around." Tessa nodded in agreement.

"Well I don't care about the time frame," spoke Colton. "I would feel better about going around." Tom and Jeb both approved his affirmation.

Rick scowled at Colton. He knew exactly what kind of a man he was. At this moment he would have loved to slap the cuffs on him but now was not the time. He knew Colton had to be wanted somewhere, he could feel it. The deciding factor came from behind them when the sound of an angry roar echoed over the land, sending an ominous feeling through the group even though the source was miles away. Without hesitating they moved forward, toward the grazing herds. They did not get far when Rick's cell phone beeped. Glancing at the text while walking Rick suddenly swore, causing the group to stop and look at him.

"Ramon says he lost connection to the servers and the website is down."

Tessa thought that was great. "Isn't that what we wanted?"

"Not until we were off the island in case any of the dinosaurs broke free of the arena. With no power to those servers there is nothing stopping the gates from those holding pens opening on their own. That one dinosaur breaking out did not help."

Tessa's face paled. "Maybe they won't find the opening right away."

"By what we just heard at least one has. We have got to keep moving."

In a short time they were in the middle of a herd of Hadrosaurs, trying to be as quiet as possible so as not to spook them. While they walked Rick noted Dixie-May's jewelry. Not only were the bracelets making some noise, the sun's rays were hitting them, as well as her earrings making them glitter. The animals shifted somewhat, acting a little skittish. They were obviously nervous. Most moved away as the group approached while a few settled down enough to munch a few blades of grass.

A moment later they were clear of the huge dinosaurs only to find themselves surrounded by a group of small dinosaurs with thin legs, long, stiff tails and about four feet long. They were definitely stream-lined for running and an insatiable degree of curiosity. Once again Dixie-May's jewelry was the center of that curiosity. Being close to the height of a German Sheppard the small animals would run around them, zipping in and out. When one would catch the reflective gleam of a bracelet it would reach up to toy with the circlet. Several times Dixie-May had to brush or swat one of them away.

As Rick watched Dixie-May's struggle he reflected on the small plant eater's reactions. While they walked he also saw some of them jump at brightly colored insects. They were mistaking her bracelets for the bugs. A few moments later the animals moved on. Rick noticed Dixie-May was limping.

"Miss Summers, why are you limping? Are you hurt?"

Dixie-May turned to look at Rick. "No, I am not hurt. My shoe's heal on my right foot broke off."

"There are a couple of small boulders a little to your right. Make your way over there so we can have a look."

Limping over to the boulders Dixie-May leaned against the lower of the two. Unlacing her shoe she handed it to Rick, along with the broken heal. Rick arched a brow. "I need the other shoe."

Perplexed Dixie-May removed her other shoe. Once in Rick's hand he quickly snapped the shoes heal off then handed both shoes back to her. She stared at them, dumbfounded, and then her temper flared. "Do you know how much I paid for these?!"

"It doesn't matter what you paid. Your life is more important. You also need to take that jewelry off."

Dixie-May stared at him, not believing his insolent manner. "I will not!"

Tom Colony had been pacing around the group, his impatience quite evident, stopped suddenly to face Dixie-May. "You are a walking dinner bell lady, take-them-off!"

Dixie-May gave him a scathing look as she put her shoes back on. Once they were laced she reached for her earrings. Placing them inside a pocket she reached for one of the bracelets when a sudden loud noise made everyone turn to look.

A herd of Pentaceratops had been grazing nearby when two of them broke off from the group to lock horns in battle. The huge power of the animals was quite evident as they struggled, dirt and sand swirling at their feet while other dinosaurs moved out of their way.

The group watched for a bit, awestruck when Jeb caught sight of another dinosaur running at the two fighters. His blood chilled when the animal appeared over top of one of the Pentaceratops, clamping its jaws over the back while long taloned claws dug into its side. The Pentaceratop screamed in rage and pain as he arched his head back, sweeping with the large shield covering his neck in an attempt to push the aggressor away. The other Pentaceratop stepped back, bellowing a warning call while its opponent weakened rapidly. From that point pandemonium reined as other alarm warnings echoed over the land, sending the animals in a panic run from all directions.

The sudden appearance of the Spinosaurus put the group on sudden alert as well. Securing themselves behind the boulders they kept a watchful eye on the carnivore until the stampede receded somewhat. Then one by one they faded away toward the trees, allowing the animal to feed. Once safely within each one ran until they could run no more.

After a brief time to rest they set out again. As the trees and foliage encircled them they felt a bit more secure. Tessa figured it was close to noon since the sun's rays penetrated through the branches directly above them. When the group came upon a small stream Rick and Tessa knew they were close to the helicopter. Before crossing they checked to see if it were safe. All they could see was a Stegosaurus a short way down quietly eating some of the green foliage and ferns growing along side. Deciding it was safe enough they made their way across, taking time to drink the cool, clear liquid from the stream.

* * * * *

The Saurophaganax looked at the strange creature that did not move. Stretching his neck forward and raising his head he roared, exposing long blade-like teeth to intimidate. When this was not successful he paced back and forth, giving the silent creature a sideways glance before it roared again.

At the forests edge, concealed and safe for the moment Rick, Tessa and the others watched the animal. Each took a personal note of the helicopter's condition. So far it looked to be unharmed. If they did not do something soon their only means of escape could be destroyed within seconds.

"Okay, any bright ideas as to how we can get that, that whatever it is away from here?"

Everyone looked at Tom Colony. Tessa was not overly impressed with his attitude. "The animal is called a Saurophaganax."

Lester Colton moved forward to get a better view. "Well, to me it looks like a huge, oversized Allosaurus."

Dixie-May looked at the animal with wide eyes. "Look at those claws. They are close to, if not as long as the Spinos."

Jeb visibly shuttered. "Don't remind me."

While the others discussed the dinosaur Rick's mind was rolling through possible ideas until he settled for one. They could not wait for the animal to wonder away by itself. The Saurophaganax could, at any moment attack the machine, in which case the animal could possibly get hurt while killing their only chance of getting off the island. Rick chose the only option. "We are going to have to lure him away."

Heads turned in Rick's direction. Tom was the first to speak. "Just how do you propose to do that?"

"By using something he would be interested in. Live bait comes to mind."

Tom looked worried. "You don't expect one of us?"

"I was thinking of myself really. I am a good runner and I am hoping, when I hit the trees to get far enough ahead of him to hide in the bushes. This will give everyone the time they need to get to the chopper."

"Do you know how lame that sounds? That animal can run faster than a man. There is no way you can out run it!"

Rick looked at Tessa, noting the worried expression on her face. He knew that look very well. She saw through him, knowing this was a suicide mission. "Yes I know, but it is all we have."

"I don't like the idea at all. Why don't we just wait the animal out?"

"I understand but we need to get him away from the chopper. We can't afford the possibility of him harming it." Addressing the others Rick continued, "What I need you to do is to stay here while I make my way around." Pointing to an area across from them, "I will come out over there. Once the animal follows me and disappears into the trees I want you to get to the helicopter."

As soon as the others agreed to his terms Rick moved to leave, stopping with the light touch on his arm. Looking up his eyes locked with Tessa's. "Come back to me." He smiled, understanding, and then he was gone.

* * * * *

A short way into the woods Laura and Bradley found themselves on a trail. A small wooden sign soon told them they were headed for the harbor. Keeping to the trail proved interesting at one point as they had to skirt around a grazing Mussaurus, a small long-necked dinosaur ten feet long and three feet tall. She seemed docile enough but the claws on her feet seemed quite impressive. She obviously used them to defend herself.

Once they passed her by the going was easy enough. When the smell of the ocean reached them Laura and Bradley knew they were close. They both felt confident in reaching their goal when a commotion to their right elicited a startled cry from Laura and sent Bradley to the ground in a crumbled heap. Dazed for a moment at the sudden change Laura looked at her husband lying on the ground then up into the eyes of J.T. His lip curled in a sneer. "You stupid bitch, I could have given you anything you wanted! You have ruined everything. You will pay for this." Springing forward he grabbed her, but she jerked free of his grasp and ran. Trees spun past her in a blur, her one main goal was to put distance between herself and J.T. in order to reach the boat in the hope of finding a weapon. She did not break her stride, even when she broke free of the woods into a clearing. Only when she felt J.T.'s hands clasp over her shoulder and arm did she know her goal was thwarted. As she felt herself being pulled back she went with it. Whirling around with all the force she could muster Laura brought her hand out to connect with his cheek, digging her fingernails in, leaving a crimson trail. J.T. recoiled at the sudden stinging pain. Reaching his hand up to touch his cheek he felt the wet, sticky evidence of blood.

His face contorted in rage. Snarling he lunged for her only to be grabbed from behind. Having no time to react at the sudden change he had a brief glance of the fist before it contacted with his nose, the impact causing him to bleed while the force knocked him to the ground.

Looking up he made eye contact with Bradley's narrowed gaze. Not saying a word he tentatively touched his nose to see if it were broken. Blood trickled from his nose and lip into his mouth, causing him to spit it out. His features again showed evident anger as he rose to his feet to lunge at Bradley. A sudden movement to his right stopped his forward motion, freezing him in place. Bradley also froze, realizing they were no longer alone.

It was at that moment Laura heard the clicking sound, not soft but commanding, as one coming from an alpha female. Laura looked up from the fight, seeing for the first time the raptors that now encircled them. Gazing past her husband she saw the mother raptor standing close to a male Raptor, obviously her new alpha male. Laura quickly answered her in kind, nodding her head in acknowledgement. Walking over to Bradley Laura took his hand, guiding him to take their place beside the mother raptor, leaving J.T. in the center.

Once Laura stood in her proper place of rank as a pack member the full impact of what she and Bradley had just done hit her. They had inadvertently passed sentence on J.T. Now it was up to the mother raptor to pass the final judgment.

The alpha female moved forward, confident in her position. She and her newly formed pack members had come upon the fight scene between the two-leggers after having fed from a recent kill. Her senses were on alert when she saw the two-legger who had killed her previous life mate, once again attacking another one of her own. Moving forward she almost intervened but stopped when she saw the female two-legger's mate stride up to take control. The moment he made the final decision as to the cruel two-legger's sentence she was clear to approach. Now, as she studied the markings she knew the decision was just. This one was a threat to her family, and any threat needed to be dealt with immediately.

J.T. did not like the way things were going and was feeling anxious. When the Raptor moved toward him he wanted to turn and run but couldn't. He looked to Laura and Bradley for answers. Bradley looked a bit confused as Laura shook her head, and then looked down. There was nothing she could do for him now. As she stood there she remembered her time spent with the pack as she studied them, learning the ways they governed themselves. Their rules and regulations were geared toward the preservation of their families. In this case, when only two members of the pack who were not alphas passed sentence on another the alpha female decided if the decision had merit, then, depending on the severity of the offense, the type of punishment, exile or death, was applied. For this type of decision the alpha male did not have to take part.

The alpha female finished her inspection of J.T. then walked back to her place beside her mate. Laura looked at Bradley. Taking his hand she held it for comfort and support as the pack moved toward J.T.

* * * * *

As Rick moved into the clearing he noted that the Saurophaganax was sniffing at one of the tail rotors. Continuing to move forward Rick could feel the distance from the confining trees. Five feet, ten feet, what was he thinking? He was walking toward death and he knew it. So what was the difference between this and his job? Facing death was an ongoing process with his profession. Somehow the thought of facing criminals was a bit different than facing an animal that could tear you to shreds.

Rick abruptly stopped at the sudden snap of a twig. The Saurophaganax turned to look in Rick's direction. Not bothering to see if the animal moved Rick turned and ran for the trees. Feeling the earth pound with each step the dinosaur took was the only evidence telling him that the animal followed close behind. It was enough to push him into high gear, the adrenaline kicking in. Adrenaline was like that. You could travel on the fumes.

Rick knew his goal, an area he had picked out earlier and he headed straight for it. Entering the woods he quickly found the place and hid. Holding his breath he waited. Within seconds the Saurophaganax stood near his place of concealment. Even though he wasn't a very religious person Rick prayed that the animal could not smell him, that he was down wind. A moment later the Saurophaganax roared in frustration. He walked a few feet past Rick's hiding place when he stopped. A strange sound reached him. Intrigued he quickly located the directional source. Turning around he walked back toward the clearing. Rick heard it too and silently cursed. Damn Dixie-May and those bracelets.

Quickly leaving his hiding place he followed the dinosaur. Reaching the clearing just seconds after the Saurophaganax Rick was able to see the others as they made a running dash for the chopper. The dinosaur was barreling down on them fast, which didn't give Rick very much time. Racing forward he shouted as loud as he could. Reaching for his semi automatic he unsheathed it and fired the weapon into the air. This got the animal's immediate attention. He snarled at Rick, moving a step toward him. Stopping he looked again at the fleeing figures. For a moment it looked as though he was going for them but he suddenly pivoted, making a dash for Rick.

With barely enough time to react Rick turned to run. As he did his foot caught on a patch of grass. He fell with a thud, the breath knocked from him. Behind him Tessa screamed.

Rolling onto his back Rick looked up at the Saurophaganax. At that point everything moved in slow motion as Rick watched the jaws open, snarling first then opening wider while descending downward. Rick's gaze focused on the teeth, long and sharp, like small blades. So intent was his perusal the sound of a loud, angry roar did not register at first. When the jaws suddenly closed, then to rise upward did he realize they were no longer alone? Rising up on his elbows Rick looked over his shoulder. Only when the Saurophaganax bellowed loudly in answer to the threat did Rick see the Spinosaurus.

Taking quick advantage of the dinosaur's distraction Rick got to his feet and ran toward the helicopter just as the two animals clashed in battle. Reaching the door he flung it open, literally falling inside. Hands quickly reached for him, helping him to his feet. The moment he did he found himself suddenly encased in a bear hug as Tessa held him close, momentarily forgetting herself. She did not care. When she saw him fall she went ballistic, attempting to run to his aide. It took all three men to hold her back. Now, as she pulled back to look at him she felt her cheeks flush. She quickly composed herself, hoping Rick had not noticed.

Stationed away from the couple Lester Colton watched them through narrowed eyes. He had noticed quite a bit while Rick made his way to the helicopter. He remained silent while everyone regrouped.

"Does anyone know how to fly this thing? Tom Colony looked worried as he studied the others for a reassuring answer. Dixie-May looked outside, trying to ascertain how much time they had. At the moment both animals were threatening each other with bellowing roars, circling while looking for an opening to strike; both aware of their lethal weapons.

Jeb volunteered, "I can fly an airplane, but I am afraid that flying a helicopter is different."

Catching his breath Rick moved toward the controls. During his career as a street patrol officer he had spent three years of five with the San Diego's Air Support Unit referred to as ABLE (Air Borne Law Enforcement) before rotating back to the streets. He wanted that experience so he could work toward a permanent position as a pilot. One of the qualifications was the possession of a private fixed wing license with thirty hours of pilot in command time, which he also possessed. Now this knowledge would save their lives.

"Don't go any farther Mr. Chavez, or whoever you are."

Rick froze, and then turned to look at Lester Colton. His jaw tightened, eyes narrowing slightly as he took in the lethal position of the man and the Berretta Colton now aimed in his direction.

Outside the battle ensued causing the ground to shake. Their time was quite limited.

"Lester, what are you doing?" Dixie-May was shocked.

"Shut up woman. You of all people should know that I don't take kindly to those who have a gun without my knowledge. I get very nervous."

"I assure you, my husband only carries it for protection."

"So do cops. How do I know that you both are not cops?" he then moved the gun to include Tessa, and then back to Rick. The moment he did someone from behind grabbed his wrist, pushing it toward the floor. Colton tensed, struggling to release himself and regain control of the weapon. Tom Colony held on, refusing to give in. When he saw his opening he took it. With his right hand forming a fist he brought it up to connect with Colton's face. The force of the blow knocked Colton backward causing his finger to catch. When the gun fired everyone jumped.

For a moment no one moved. Seeing the gun lying on the floor Tessa picked it up, took the clip out and placed the weapon out of the way. She looked at Colton sitting against the wall, rubbing his jaw while glaring at Tom. Shaking her head she turned to look at Rick. He smiled at her then said, "I'm not going to be able to fly us out after all."

Tessa looked puzzled for a moment then her eyes grew round when she saw a circle of red form and spread on his upper shoulder, staining his blue denim shirt. She rushed over to him as Rick slumped to the floor. Jeb, Tom, and Dixie-May soon joined her.

"Is he going to be, Okay?" Dixie-May was angry at Lester for shooting the nice man.

"It looks like the bullet went straight through his shoulder," Tessa remarked as she examined the wound.

Looking at Tessa and Rick Tom asked, "What do you mean you can't fly us out of here?"

Tessa looked at Tom, exhaustion evident on her face. "He said exactly what he meant. In order to fly a helicopter, you have to use both hands and feet. Being shot makes him incapable of flying."

"Then how the hell are we getting out of here?! There has to be someone who can fly this thing." For a while no one spoke.

"I can fly us out."

Everyone turned their heads in the direction of the voice. Lester Colton moved forward. Ignoring their glares, he continued, "I have a license and over thirty hours of fly time. Get your husband strapped in Mrs. Chavez, we are taking off." Moving past the suspicious looks and a concerned Tessa, Colton sat in the control seat.

Tessa rushed to get Rick seat-belted into a cushioned seat while the others found their own. Dixie-May sat at a window to see the progress of the fight even though they could hear and feel the scuffle. Looking closely at the two dinosaurs Dixie-May could see the fight was about over. Both showed signs of tiring, with each having their share of cuts and slashes, although the Spinosaurus seemed to have the most. As Colton flipped the switch, starting the helicopter's engine and the rotor blades to turn the Saurophaganax pivoted just as the Spino lunged at him. Quick on its feet the Sauroph finished the spin by ramming the Spino on its side. Weakened form loss of blood and taken off balance the Spino fell. Landing on his side his back snapped when the sail hit the ground. Being fused to his vertebrae the break was inevitable and death quickly followed. The Sauroph moved into feed until he became aware of another creature, one that had been quiet. Looking toward the chopper he roared causing Dixie-May's eyes to widen in fear.

Keeping the rotor disc level Colton pulled on the collective, allowing the pitch in the rotor blades to increase equally as the helicopter rose. It seemed forever for Dixie-May and the others as they saw the Sauroph step over the Spino and charge toward the chopper. Even weakened from the fight the animal seemed to be moving on adrenaline. Ten feet into the air everyone was jolted as the animal rammed the chopper, pushing it off balance. Dixie-May screamed as Colton worked to return the chopper's balance while rising a few more feet. Constantly adjusting the controls to maintain his height, position and direction he hovered for a bit. Satisfied Colton pushed the cyclic forward, which caused the rotor disk to tilt forward, resulting in the nose of the chopper slanting down, pushing the helicopter forward. As it did the Sauroph jumped, snapping its jaws in an attempt to grab and hold. Narrowly missing the jaws connected with just air, causing the animal to roar in frustration and anger. Whipping its tail from side-to-side it soon returned to the Spinosaurus.

* * * * *

As the chopper moved safely away Tessa looked at Rick. He was barely awake. She knew they had to get him to a hospital, and but quick. She also worried over Laura and Bradley Sinclair. Where were they and how could they possibly find them now? Somehow, she felt she had failed them. At that moment Dixie-May shouted, "Look everyone, look; down there!"

Tessa, Jeb, and Tom allowed their gaze to follow Dixie-May's pointing finger. Tessa smiled. Below them was a boat, a fancy one heading in the direction of Costa Rica. At the helm was Bradley Sinclair and giving them an enthusiastic wave was Laura. After the incident with J.T. the mother raptor walked the rest of the way with Laura and Bradley to the shore where J.T.'s private boat was anchored. Laura was happy her friend had made a new life for herself here. She obviously did not have to go back to the other island, nor did she want to. The mother raptor's life was here now. Once Laura made it back to the mainland, she would see to it that this island, like the other two would be made as a wildlife reserve, off limits to other people. These animals deserved to live in peace. After all, the mother raptor and herself were both mothers and the two most important things in their lives were their children and soul mates. Both added up to complete a united family. There could be nothing better.

* * * * *

The next morning Sam Bentley sat in his kitchen enjoying a steaming cup of coffee while watching the news. It was just mundane information to him, accidents with vehicles, one bank robbery, the supposedly predictable weather, and sport scores with highlights. Soon his mind began to wander about the coming day. It was his day off so he planned to work on his favorite hobby. Thinking of it he barely heard the newscaster until she said one word that quickly brought his full attention back to the screen, "ebony."

"Another island has been sealed off by the Costa Rican government. It was reported by well known author and veterinarian Laura Sinclair that the island known as Isle Ebony has been found to contain dinosaurs and is now being declared a natural wildlife reserve for them. Most if not all of the animals had been released due to a power failure since some had been held in holding pens." A minute later, after listening to the reasons behind the holding pens Sam reached over to turn off the set. For a moment he just stared at the blank screen. Now it would seem that he had no job. He so enjoyed working in the hatchery.

Picking up his empty coffee mug he took it over to the sink, rinsed it and set it down. Pausing briefly he gazed out the bay window at the scenic view. The sun was almost up now, sending bright rays of light over the landscape. Beautiful he thought. His mind soon wandered again as he remembered his hours spent working in the hatchery and the animals it had contained. They were all beautiful animals and he enjoyed spending time with them. There had been two pits, one containing a young pair of T-Rex, male and female. The other pit contained a female Nanotyrannus. They had hoped to mate her with the adult Nano.

There was several egg patches, nests kept warm under an overhead lamp hung from the ceiling. When the eggs hatched the nestlings were put in a tiny pit which was also kept warm by hanging lamps. Several Allosaurus were in one. Another contained two Dryptosaurus. Now they were all on their own. Once the power failed a safety mechanism started the backup to release the cages and the floor of the pits rose up to allow the dinosaurs to escape.

Leaving the kitchen Sam made his way to the garage. He would miss his job very much. Opening a door built into the inside wall he passed through onto a landing. Taking the stairs he walked down a hall to another door. Entering he flipped a light switch then gazed in awe of his own hatchery. He had always been a science buff. When he heard about the job he applied right away even though he did not have to worry about money. He was a very wealthy man, owning the mansion he now lived in. His Escazu home in Costa Rica offered everything he needed for being a recluse. A scenic view of the mountains and valley, in a nature surrounded environment. Complete with four bedrooms and seven bathrooms, swimming pool, Jacuzzi and plenty of space to use your imagination. Space that he put to good use for the safety enclosed out buildings housed his own collection of dinosaurs. There had been quite a few eggs at the island hatchery so if one just suddenly disappeared no one noticed.

Smiling Sam walked into his hatchery to check on a new batch of eggs due to hatch soon. Looking down into the nest he was elated to see two pecking their way out, a tiny Velociraptor and a Nanotyrannus.

PART THREE

A FATHER'S LOVE FOR THAT OF THE MOTHER

The scream sliced through the silence of the night, causing Sam Bentley to jump from the comfort of his bed and race down to the secret basement where he kept the Raptors confined. 'Damn those Raptors,' he thought. 'They were nothing but a nuisance. Always trying to find ways to get out.' He wished he had never brought their eggs to his home.

The room he now entered had once been a hatchery but was converted for the Raptors since he had run out of the eggs he had brought over from Ebony Island a year ago. He had thought there would be more eggs when the animals matured, but that was not happening fast enough as he was running out of the dinosaurs as well. The plant eaters, whom he had let roam the grounds were decreasing due to using them to feed his Nanos and Raptors as well as a strange disease that almost wiped out his population. He was sure he had it in check, but once in a while he would find one suddenly dying. This took its toll, not allowing time for the animals to catch up so they can lay eggs. On rare moments he would find a nest of eggs, but most would never hatch and if one did the hatchling would not survive long.

What also amazed him was the fact that the meat eaters were not affected by the disease. They ate the plant eaters with no signs or symptoms to their health, although it did reflect toward their egg laying. There wasn't as many as he felt there should be.

Looking into the cage where his young Raptors huddled in a far corner he quickly counted them. All five were there. He frowned then. Why did they act so scared? Their eyes darting to and fro as they looked beyond him. It was then he heard a noise coming from behind him. As he turned he suddenly wished he had checked his monitors before coming down here. A second later, another scream broke through the silence of the night to be cut short, allowing the night to continue its silent vigil.

Two Months Later

Cassie Reynolds thought she was in heaven right now. An hour and a half into their riverboat wildlife cruise she was enjoying the sight of so many beautiful birds. There were Great Curassows, Scarlet Macaws, White Ibis, Roseate Spoonbills, Ankingas, Jabirus and Wood Storks. Being an avid bird watcher, she had studied up on the bird population of Costa Rica so she could easily identify them. Her ten year old daughter Sari, on the other hand was enjoying the scenery, an occasional animal sighting, which happened frequently and the frequent appearance of White-faced Monkeys who took it upon themselves to come aboard for small treats and because they were just curious.

Both sat in a twenty-three seat boat that reminded Cassie of a large oversized row boat with an out-board motor attached to the back end. She estimated the boat was at least twenty feet long and six to ten feet wide. Above them was a huge canopy that covered the entire boat, shielding them from the relentless rays of the hot sun.

Because of the heat Cassie wore a pair of tan shorts with a white tank top. A small pair of binoculars hung from her neck to mingle with a necklace, which had a locket on the end containing two small pictures of her daughter, one when she was just a babe and the other taken before they left on this trip. The picture revealed her daughter's long blonde hair flowing over her shoulders, disappearing down her back. Her bangs framed a slim, olive face in small ringlet curls. She preferred her hair long, whereas Cassie preferred hers cut short, layered in the back, bangs shortened and the sides feathered, then brought around to frame a face similar to her daughters. The only difference, Cassie had blush added to her face to try and conceal any wrinkles threatening to make an appearance, whereas her daughter's face was unblemished and pure. Oh to be young again, although thirty-nine wasn't too bad of an age to be right now.

Cassie noticed the boat had passed through a bend or curve in the river. Their guide, Manual suddenly stopped the small vessel to give the passengers a moment or two to take pictures. For this trip there were only two other people besides Cassie and Sari. A middle-aged couple in their fifties sat across from them while all four sat in the center of the boat. She had learned their names were Frank and Millie Cooper from Missouri.

Feeling her right arm getting too warm from the sun, she set her camera down and reached for their tote bag to search for the sunscreen. At that moment the boat lurched suddenly and rose straight in the air, paused for a moment, then landed back into the water with a small splash. Everyone on board tried to regain their balance when it happened again. A short outcry came from the women as Frank cried out, "What did we hit, a crocodile?!"

At that moment Sari saw them, "Mom, look! They are dinosaurs!"

Cassie looked sharply at her daughter, and then turned to look over the water. "There are no dinosaurs in Costa _____!"

Her mother's sudden sharp intake of breath was enough to convince Sari that she was correct. All were shocked; stunned to silence except Sari as the two Nanos reached the shore, shaking themselves off any excess water.

"See, I told you they were dinosaurs!"

The strange noise was enough to get the male Nano's attention, causing him to turn and look toward the direction of the source. At that moment the slight breeze changed direction and he caught their scent. The animal roared loudly, the sound thundering over the water, causing the occupants of the boat to move into action as the two Nanos entered the water again.

Manuel quickly moved to start the engine while reaching down to pick up a club he kept near his seat in case a wayward croc decided to try climbing into the boat. He turned the key, nothing. He tried again, nothing. It could not be flooded he thought.

"Please, for the love of God start the engine," cried Frank.

"Hurry!" Shouted Millie and Cassie in unison.

"Mr. Cooper! I need you to take this club and hit them on the nose if they try to get aboard!"

Frank looked at him as though he had gone mad, but it was enough of a hesitation for Sari to reach for and grab a hold of it just as the boat started to tip and the ladies started screaming. Sari turned in time to see the male Nanotyrannus reach the boat first. Swinging the club, she hit the animal with all the power and strength her small body could muster, connecting with the soft nose of the animal. The Nano cried out in pain and anger, releasing the boat and falling back into the water. The sudden release of the boat caused Sari to lose her balance. At that moment Sari saw the female, with open jaws below her as the animal propelled itself out of the water to grab the tasty morsel. Sari, even though she was falling, swung the club again in an attempt to defend herself, striking the female in the upper jaw. At that moment two other things happened. Cassie, seeing that her daughter was about to fall reached out to grab her, pulling her back to safety, just as the motor of the boat kicked in. Manuel quickly pushed the boat to as high as 115hp would let them go.

Cassie held her daughter close as they left the two Nanos behind. Sari hugged her mom to reassure her that she was all right then sat in her seat. After they traveled a good mile Sari noticed something on the floor of the boat. Reaching down she picked it up and held the object so she could observe it better.

"Mother look, it's the tooth from that dinosaur."

Cassie looked at it as though it had a life of its own. She shuddered, thinking of what that tooth and the others with it could have done to her daughter, to all of them.

* * * * *

The sun peaked through the thick clouds, trying to push its warm rays to reach the land below. It quickly lost its fight as the clouds moved in, darkening the day. Flashes of light briefly lit the sky. The sound of thunder soon followed.

'What a gloomy day this is turning out to be,' thought Laura as the rain began to pelt the ground outside and run from the eaves of her home. Turning back to her living room, she made her way through the house to the garage, checking briefly on her son. She watched him for a moment as he slept, noting how he cuddled his favorite stuffed elephant close to him. Now he was so quiet and peaceful than when awake. Then he was like a live wire, so full of energy. Always wanting to climb, run, jump or throw things. He was always curious, wanting to explore his world. This meant trying to turn a few doorknobs, which meant the addition of child proof locks placed on certain doors in the kitchen.

Looking up, she nodded briefly and smiled at the babysitter sitting in the corner with a small lamp and a good book. That brought back the memory of last night. As she walked to her car she recalled reading a book to her son who enjoyed listening to her voice. He enjoyed having books read to him.

After parking her car in her reserved parking slot of the San Diego Zoo she reached in her purse for her cell phone, wanting to call Bradley to see if he would like to meet her for dinner. When she could not find it, she started to panic, trying to think of where she had it last. She relaxed shortly after when she realized she had left it sitting on her night stand. No problem as she could just call him from her office.

Several hours later, Laura reclined with her husband in the family room were they both enjoyed a friendly game of darts.

"You did not just do that, did you?" Bradley questioned.

Laura smiled as she looked at the small dart protruding from the center of the board.

"Not fair! You don't even throw them right."

"Oh, you are just being a sore loser."

"Mistress Sinclair...?"

Both turned when they heard the voice of their housekeeper and close friend, Rosa.

"There is a phone call for you. I was tidying up in your room when your cell phone rang so I answered it. I hope that was all right? He said it was very urgent and has been trying to call you all day."

"That is fine Rosa. I remember one of the interns had taken a call while I was in surgery. She could barely understand him, he was talking so fast. Thank you."

Rosa handed her the phone and left the room.

Bradley watched his wife as she took the call. When her posture stiffened he frowned. Shortly after she hung up the phone and turned to face him. He was taken aback by the pale, ashen look on her face.

"What is it?" He probed.

* * * * *

Several hours later, Laura and Bradley landed at the Palmar Sur airport in Costa Rica. It was a quick and hasty trip of trying to pack, make arrangements for their son to be taken care of and seeing that someone was left in charge of the San Diego Zoo veterinarian's clinic to handle affairs while she was away. By the time they boarded the plane they were both quite tired and slept for most of the flight. Now, as they rode to where Sam Bentley had made his home, she feared what she might find there.

So far the trip to Bentley's place of residence was pretty nice. Since they would be traveling in the mountains the temperature ranged in the seventies. Being near the pacific coast temperatures varied by about seven to ten degrees throughout the year, which was Laura's favorite temperature range. They traveled on a paved two lane road that soon changed to unpaved as they progressed further into the mountains. Following a curve in the road they came out into a small valley, complete with a lake and lots of vegetation. To Laura it looked as though it had once been a crater left by a long dead volcano.

The road twisted and turned its way down toward the bottom, which wasn't very far until it came to an abrupt stop, suddenly finding themselves faced with a huge thirty to fifty foot tall gate connected to the walls of the same height. Immediately Laura was brought back to another time when she first entered the walls of Ebony Island. This was almost an exact duplicate of the construction, although the name was different. As they drove through the now open gate the words 'Bentley's Sanctuary' looked down upon them. After they passed through, the gates closed with a resounding thud, adding emphasis to the fact they were now locked within.

They were quickly greeted by several interactive scenes. The first that drew both Laura and Bradley's attention was the panoramic scene of the lake. It was breathtaking. Crystal clear blue water sparkled from the suns rays. The lake was surrounded by areas of grass, trees and in the distance a steep wall of mountains like cliffs. A wall built by nature.

The next scene was the many dinosaurs milling around the edge of the lake or swimming within its depths. Most of them, if not all were quite young adolescents. Laura frowned, thinking it odd. For as long as the animals had been here they should be close to, if not at adult age. Years ago, when the animals were first introduced those who worked in the labs had given each of the hatchlings a growth formula with their regular food. To the application of each batch of hatchlings the effects of the formula were passed on throughout the years, allowing the animals to grow at a faster rate. This helped to bring about all three islands. At that moment three full grown Hadrasaurs and two Brachiosaurus emerged from behind a stand of trees. The Brachiosaurus headed for the water while the Hadrasaurs began to graze. Something seemed odd about their movement, but Laura could not put a finger on it.

Following the narrow driveway, they approached the house located to their left and facing the lake and its inhabitants. Laura was awestruck as to the immense size of the building, truly more of a mansion than anything. A bay window overlooked the mountains and the valley below them. Later she would learn of the four bedrooms, seven bathrooms, swimming pool and an open kitchen, which led into the dining room and living room. Both of them took note of the out buildings surrounding the main house and the intense activity around them. As they parked the car they were quickly met by a man who raced up to greet them.

He introduced himself as Frank Mandela. Short cropped dark hair sat against a fair-skinned complexion, emphasizing his European bloodline. He smiled, showing white teeth exposed under a dark, precisely trimmed mustache. Eyes bright and alert he took her hand stating, "Pure Vida." Laura returned the greeting.

A little while later both Laura and Bradley were given a tour and brought up to date on what was going on. It seemed they had discovered this dinosaur hideaway when Mr. Bentley had not picked up his mail, which resulted in the contents piling up. At first they hesitated to send someone out as Bentley stressed the fact no one was too special deliver anything. They finally broke down when the contents were too much to bear. She was also informed on the condition of the dinosaurs. For the rest of that day Laura spent her time in the lab, researching, going over notes left by Bentley. Even now, as her husband slept beside her, she read and re-read the notes, jotting down little messages of her own in the margins.

One area that drew out her curiosity was the carnivores having small abdomens, which did not require large digestive systems resulting in their swallowing their food whole. They were also used to eating rancid meat since their systems were made for it. The herbivores had large abdomens, which meant they stored large amounts of vegetation for a long time that it takes the vegetation to digest. She also remembered reading an article in a science magazine about the dinosaurs on the first island getting sick every six months and they had never been able to solve it. Laura wondered if it was related somehow to what was happening here. Either way the dinosaurs in Bentley's Sanctuary would not be able to be transferred to Ebony Island until the problem was solved. While this was being looked into by the staff it would leave her open to solve another problem, that of finding the Velociraptors.

A few hours later Bradley returned from the bathroom to see his wife had fallen asleep with a number of papers strewn about on the bed. Smiling while shaking his head, he quietly picked the papers up, placing them on the nightstand. Then he tenderly tucked her arms under the covers and watched as she snuggled down further, moaning a bit, then muttering the word 'mother.' Crawling under the covers he snuggled close to her and fell asleep.

* * * * *

The five Raptors drank from a stream fed by a waterfall, surrounded by one of many untouched forests of Costa Rica. This suited the Raptors quite well. They felt secure and safe in its lush, dense foliage. Now, as they moved out to hunt, the forest worked to conceal them from their prey.

* * * * *

"Are you sure this is a good idea?"

Bradley watched his wife as she packed some things into a backpack.

"It is the only thing I can think of. What better ways to find Raptors than to have a Raptor call them? Plus, we will be able to find them faster."

"True, but there is the fact that it is not their mating season as it was the last time you were there so you will be taking a big chance, even though you are a member of the pack. Will they remember that?"

Laura knew this to be true, but she had no choice in the matter. It was a chance she was going to have to take.

A few hours later, after driving thirty miles to the pier in Palmar Sur, boarding the small vessel they were coming up to Ebony Island. Laura and Bradley studied the beach, looking for any type of movement or signs of life. Deciding it was safe enough Laura made sure her backpack was secure and the knife belt strapped to her waist. Since she had used a knife to help the mother raptor and herself escape harm the last time she had been on an island where dinosaurs were present her viewpoint of weapons had changed. Now her belt contained, in their respective sheaths looped onto the belt several throwing knives, each having stainless steel blades, double edged and sharp. Attached to the outside of her backpack were three tactical survival knives with partially serrated, combo edged fixed blades. In close, hand to hand combat she had an abomination fifteen-inch survival knife with a blade fixed length of ten inches was placed within easy reach from her backpack. Before she bought them, she had tested each one to make sure they fit comfortably in her hand, that they were the right size blade with full tang, and a sharp pointed tip to effectively thrust a stab; all to give the self-defense she needed.

Now, standing on the beach she hoped it would be enough. Facing the forest, she sent out a call to the pack. It was a call the mother raptor would recognize. Silence followed. A moment passed and she repeated the call. As she heard the distant bellowing of a dinosaur in response she saw movement near the forest's edge. It was at that moment she heard the return call and the mother raptor appeared with four others, a hunting pack. Laura glanced over her shoulder to see Bradley poised with a rifle, ready to fire if the need arose. Laura signed a greeting to the mother raptor then took a submissive stance in accordance to an alpha's rank and her position as a pack member. The mother raptor accepted her greeting by responding with a sharp bark, and then turned back toward the forest. Laura followed, as did the rest of the pack, except one. The Raptor watched the pack disappear, and then turned to look at Bradley as he stood up from his crouched position on the boat. She hissed at him menacingly and turned to follow the pack. Bradley sensed that was not a good sign,

A couple hours later, Laura was relishing her time with the pack, reacquainting her with a few of the hatchlings, which were now quite the adult size. She was impressed that they had remembered some of the sign language she had taught them. She was also able to communicate her concern with finding the lost Raptors and the importance of having the mother raptor's help. The mother raptor agreed with a resounding bark.

All the while that Laura had been there, she always kept a wary eye out for any signs of danger. There was no telling what form it could come in. A moment later it appeared with the sound of a challenge call from one of the female raptors. The mother raptor immediately stood up from her resting position, alert and on guard, answering the challenge with a low-sounding hiss. The other Raptors scattered, and Laura stood up beside a tree as the Raptor that had stayed back on the beach now stood in front of the mother raptor, challenging her for the right to rule.

Each circled the other, looking for an opportunity to strike, an area of weakness. A series of snarls, hisses and snapping of jaws followed in an attempt to show their strength. Their front claws spread wide, claws flexing with anticipation they made several mock lunges. This type of dance went on for a good five minutes when the challenger suddenly reversed her circling. Instead of a mock charge she caught the mother raptor off guard by ramming into her side to knock her off balance and finishing the push by raking her claws down the mother raptor's side. The mother raptor screeched in pain as she landed on her side. Laura screamed as the challenger moved in for the kill. The sudden movement of the alpha male caught Laura's attention as he quickly put himself between the two in a submissive manner, emphasizing mercy as he looked at the challenger. With his side fully exposed to her sharp taloned claws he waited for her response as the new alpha female.

The challenger moved a step back in response, stood to her full height and barked several times to show her new role. The mother raptor took that opportunity to stand as Laura rushed to her side. Immediately she took her backpack, which she had never taken off and placed it on the ground. Kneeling beside it she reached for the zipper to have it suddenly snatched from her grasp. Looking up she saw the backpack dangling from the jaws of the mother raptor. She then made a partial turn as though leaving. Laura frowned, and then she remembered the other times she had witnessed the mother raptor going through the same type of challenge and being the victor, whereas the loser was exiled if shown mercy. They had to leave. Laura nodded acknowledgement then signed 'Let's get to the boat.'

The mother raptor dropped the backpack, Laura quickly snatched it up and they both took off as the new alpha watched. A few minutes after they disappeared the new alpha did something that was never done before. Searching out two of the best members of the pack she sent them after the two exiles. She would tolerate no potential rivalry, exiled or not.

Laura raced through the trees and bushes of the forest to where Bradley had moved the boat, Ebony Island's harbor. Soon she broke through the forest and found herself on the trail, which led directly to the harbor, the same trail she and Bradley had fled the island so many months ago. The mother raptor ran with her, taking it a bit slow because Laura wasn't that fast of a runner as she was a climber. But she did run. She put her heart and soul into it, not sure why but some sixth sense told her to. That sense proved true as they passed through a clearing and had their exit blocked when two Raptors rushed to obstruct their path.

The Raptors, a female and a male did not hesitate, quickly moving toward the exiles. Laura took a defense stance, quickly grabbing two of her survival knives. Laura was surprised when the female suddenly turned on her partner. Taken aback the male felt cornered as he saw the mother raptor and the young female come toward him. So intent was he on his predicament he did not see another Raptor come straight at him, landing on his back. The young male tried to role on his back in order to bring his claws up in defense but was to no avail as the alpha male quickly ended his life. When he made a move toward the female the mother raptor barked a response to stop him. The alpha male changed his course and walked over to the mother raptor, greeting her warmly by nudging her while making a strange purring type sound.

Laura was touched by his loyalty to the mother raptor, even though she was no longer the alpha female. Laura also recognized the young female as the one she had saved from a very unwanted helicopter ride when J.T.'s twin brother tried to kidnap her. Plus she was one who was quite perceptive and quick to pick up the sign language training. Laura signed to her a form of thank you. She nodded in return and left, disappearing within the trees. Briefly she wondered how the young female had gotten on the island, but knowing how J.T. had operated Laura was not surprised.

When the three of them arrived at the boat Bradley was a bit surprised to see the male Raptor tagging along. Noting the wounds on the mother raptor and Laura's quick attention to dealing with them he knew something not good had happened. He was confident Laura would fill him in later. As he started the boat he also worried about the five missing Raptors. Being hurt the way she was Bradley doubted the mother raptor would be able to help.

* * * * *

Once back at Bentley's Sanctuary everyone rested for a couple of days, giving Laura time to monitor the mother raptor's condition. She wanted to wait longer to give her wounds plenty of time to heal well but the mother raptor was restless, wanting to hunt.

The night before they left Laura sat at the kitchen table studying a map of the area where the Raptors were last reported seen, even though, at the time there were only two actually spotted.

"You are worried about her, aren't you?"

Laura looked up to watch her husband prepare a snack before sitting down beside her.

"Yes, I am. She needs to let those wounds heal well because some of them are quite deep. Truthfully I wonder how she could still be alive."

"Wasn't it you who told me once of something you read about the Theropods concerning their amazing healing abilities, how their bones could heal easily and the ability to brush off severe trauma, sickness or any subsequent signs of healing. I am sure this would apply to any injuries other than a bone fracture."

Laura had her doubts, but she so badly wanted to believe him.

"After we find the Raptors have you given any thought as to how to locate the mysterious dinosaurs Bentley referred to as his favorites?"

Laura went back to studying the map again.

"Good question." She sighed. "The only thing I can think of is to wait it out to see if someone encounters them and they report it."

Bradley got up then and put his dishes in the sink. Laura watched him, ready to tackle another issue.

"Bradley, I know you don't want to hear this but I need you to stay here."

Bradley turned to look at her, not saying anything.

"Having the two Raptors with me will help to keep the five from attacking me. It is bad enough I have to keep an eye on myself; I don't want to worry about you too. I will be okay with them."

Bradley sighed, "I don't like this idea one bit. But I suppose you know what you are doing." He came over and kissed her goodnight then left the room.

* * * * *

By the time the sun rose the next day Laura and her two companions traveled to the area where the Raptors were last seen. She knew the trail would be cold, but at least it was a starting point. As she brought the boat close to shore she let the two Raptors jump and swim ashore. After beaching the boat she followed the Raptors into the woods.

The forest was dense in spots but sparse in others. They traveled for over an hour when the male Raptor separated to search on his own. A short time later the two came across a couple of deer carcasses. While Laura examined the outer perimeter the mother raptor gulped down a few choice morsels of the now decomposing meat. This seemed promising as there were tracks a plenty and they were fresh. They had spent some time here. Going in a circular pattern Laura soon found where the five Raptors came in and left the area. Taking the same exit she followed the tracks as best she could.

After traveling a few feet she came out into another clearing. She moved to her left, traveling along the outskirts until she decided to look for the mother raptor. Stepping briefly into the clearing Laura saw her walking on the other side. Laura called to her and she responded. It was at that moment the trees and bushes behind her seemed to explode. Before she could respond she felt herself enclosed in a vice like grip, her arms pinned, and lifted into the air. Stunned at first she heard the mother raptor screech an alarm call. Laura opened her eyes at the sound to see she was in the jaws of a predator.

* * * * *

Bradley walked from one of the buildings where a few of the scientists and some lab techs worked on the disease issue. Halfway to the house he heard a car coming up the drive. He waited and watched as the car pulled up and a woman and child exited. Walking over to him they introduced themselves as Cassie and Sari Renalds.

"It is nice to meet you Mrs. Renalds. What can I do for you?"

"Please call me Cassie. My daughter insisted on coming here when she heard on the news about this dinosaur sanctuary. She wants to know if she can find out the name of the dinosaur she saw. If it were me I would rather forget the whole thing, but she is determined."

"Yes I would love to know. Is there some way to find out?" questioned Sari.

"There is a way. Come with me."

Turning back to the house Bradley took them to the library where books of all kinds lined two of the walls on oak shelves. Plush carpeting covered the floor. Several brown leather upholstered chairs and a couch were placed sporadically in the room. At the opposite wall from where they entered was a sliding glass door that led to a small balcony furnished with cushioned wicker chairs and a nightstand type table. In the center of the library was a larger table with papers and books spread over its surface, all collected information on dinosaurs.

"Why don't you look through some of the picture book ency-clopedias to find your dinosaur?" Bradley waved her to a chair and Sari took it right away, grabbing one of the books to start looking.

Bradley watched her closely, waiting for her to come to the Velociraptors, confident that she would stop at that page. He could have just told her what the animal was called, saving her the time, but he knew she had to see it to know for sure. He frowned when she passed over the Raptor page and stopped several pages from them. When Bradley looked at the animal in question he was stunned as his mind transported him back to another time and place.

"This is it. This is the dinosaur I saw," stated Sari.

"Are you positively sure?" asked Bradley, surprised he could actually find his voice.

"Yes, I am sure. The caption says it is a Nanotyrannus."

Hearing the word spoken Bradley's countenance stiffened. Noticing the change in him Cassie asked, "Are you all right Mr. Sinclair?"

"Yes, yes I am fine." He quickly composed himself. "I have to make a phone call. Please make yourself at home and I will return shortly."

* * * * *

The alpha male traveled at a steady pace, covering a good two miles before he caught a familiar scent. Following it he soon came out to a beautiful waterfall that a person could admire for its tranquility. Searching the area, he soon found what he was looking for. Lounging near the waters edge, under a tree were the five young Raptors. It did not take them long to note his appearance. They approached him cautiously at first, sniffing the air and responding with clicking noises. The alpha male greeted them in the same fashion then set about showing his dominance and authority as a leader. They responded very well and accepted him as their leader. It was, at that moment a sound reached the alpha male. His head shot up to face the direction it came, the breeze steady as it brought the sound to his ears. When it repeated the alpha male recognized it for what it was, the screeching alarm calls of his mate. He quickly answered her and took off at a fast run, the young Raptors following closely.

* * * * *

After securing her prey within her jaws the female Nano took off across the clearing but was only able to get to the center when she found herself facing a Velociraptor, one that was not going to back down. Rage filled her and she met the challenge by releasing her prey and emitting a savage roar of her own.

Once more on the ground Laura was a bit shaken but not hurt. Quickly she rebounded by jumping up. She saw the mother raptor facing the Nano. Moving in to help she catches a movement out of the corner of her eye. Turning to look Laura sees a second Nano racing to join the fight. Laura could not let that happen. Reaching for one of her knives she threw it, hoping the blade would hit its mark. When the knife sunk into the soft flesh of the Nano's neck she almost shouted out. Although it did not kill him it caused him to faultier, and then stop. Automatically he reached around for the source of the pain. In the process he saw Laura for the first time, taking on a defensive stance. He roared and charged toward her.

Laura had to be crazy, taking on a dinosaur face-to-face, but she had no time to contemplate the sanity of the moment as she took two more knives and threw them, each one hitting him in the chest. Quickly she grabbed two of the three tactical survival knives as the male Nano stopped his charge to try to dislodge the offensive object causing his pain. Looking at her he snarled, then roared revealing sharp serrated teeth and flexed his sharp taloned claws. Laura clashed the partially serrated; combo edged fixed blades of her knives and screeched at him.

Stomping his feet, the Nano lunged in a mock charge, causing Laura to hold up the knife blades in defense. Laura knew that one of the mock charges would be real. That meant her throw of the knife had to be right on for the target she aimed for. After the third mock charge the Nano came forward in a full charge. Laura took one of the knives and threw it. Then the second knife in quick succession, both landing in the neck, just under the jaw to hit the jugular. When the knives connected the Nano roared in pain and arched its head up, which offered Laura's opportunity to attack. Charging forward with the abomination fifteen-inch survival knife now in her hand she approached the Nano as he arched up and struck him, again in the neck, stabbing him deep, and then sliced his throat open. The Nano shuddered then fell to the ground.

Standing over the Nano, with knife still in hand she took a moment to catch her breath. Quickly retrieving her knives, she turned to help the mother raptor and found herself facing five others.

* * * * *

The mother raptor faced her opponent with serious determination and rage. She had never felt such rage until she saw one of her own in the jaws of her enemy. That combined with the remembrance of her first mate's death years ago was enough to warrant her rage.

The female Nano was not happy for this interruption of her hunt. She gave evidence of this by snapping her jaws, snarling and roaring to reveal her sharp serrated teeth. Both circled the other looking for an opening, a sign of weakness, each hissing and screeching. When the Nano suddenly charged forward the mother raptor was prepared. She sidestepped and pivoted, striking out with her right leg, aiming her seven-inch claw to slice the Nano's hip while sinking her teeth into the side of the soft flesh at the base of the Nano's neck. Once anchored she quickly brought up her other leg and sliced quickly at the animal's underbelly. The Nano responded by turning her head around to snap and grab the mother raptor by the back of her neck but roared in frustration and anger after her jaws clamped down on air.

Having jumped off her opponent in a quick strike and leave attack method the mother raptor raced to the other side to give the same blows when she was brought up short as the Nano suddenly turned to snap her jaws just inches from her head. Quickly the mother raptor jumped back snarling and hissing, eyes narrowing slightly. When the Nano stepped forward to snap her jaws again, trying to get the Raptor to stumble backward and fall the mother raptor emitted a high-pitched sound to intimidate the Nano not to progress further.

Ignoring her the Nano continued her onslaught but stopped suddenly when she felt weight land on her back and sharp pain emanate from the wounds already inflicted and new ones created. Glancing over her shoulder she saw the body of another Raptor. Snarling she tried to reach for him but the alpha male moved to avoid the snapping jaws. If he kept out of her reach just enough to frustrate the Nano and possibly cause her to fall over in her haste to reach him there would be no way she could get back up again. Staying out of her reach was no easy feat but it was enough of a distraction to allow the mother raptor to attack. Using all the strength she could muster she rammed into the Nano's chest. It was enough to cause the imbalance needed and the

Nano fell. Once she was down both Raptors were on her, slicing with their claws and biting chunks of flesh while avoiding the jaws and back legs of the Nano. It did not take long for her to weaken, then to lie still. They began to feed but jumped at the sound of a loud cracking noise. They looked to its source. The alpha male saw the problem and took off followed closely by the mother raptor.

* * * * *

When the five young Raptors saw another of their kind fighting one of their constant tormentors from the sanctuary they were afraid, not sure what to do. Looking to the one who led them they saw him quickly join in the fight. A bit confused as to why he would want to fight they noticed the other fight and the strange creature involved. Curiosity outweighing their fear they moved closer.

* * * * *

Laura watched the Raptors closely as she slowly moved away from the Nano, while grasping the handles of her knives in a firm grip, making sure they saw them. They could see she was a formidable opponent as she revealed her claws to them in a definite challenge. As for Laura, she was hoping they would go for the Nano carcass and leave her alone. Four of them took the offer, but the fifth one stayed its ground, deciding to take her up on the challenge. He screeched at her, flexing his claws to intimidate her. At that moment a loud cracking sound echoed over the clearing and a portion of the ground exploded under the Raptor's feet, causing the animal to jump backwards. Laura scanned the forest's edge for the shooter just as another shot rang out and the alpha male arrived. He quickly put himself between the young Raptor and Laura, chewing him out by using several distinct barking sounds. The young Raptor stepped back again, taking a submissive stance. The mother raptor joined her mate to assert her role in this new found pack. Laura's eyes soon located the source of the shooting as she watched her husband walk up to the group. She held him close for a moment, relishing in his nearness. Pulling back a bit she looked up at him.

"How did you find me?"

"You really did not think I would let you go alone, do you? I planted a device in your backpack that allowed me to track your whereabouts so I knew where you were at all times."

"I should really be angry with you, but glad that you care so much."

"Care, I love you woman!" With those words he kissed her.

* * * * *

That night both Laura and Bradley sat on a balcony from their bedroom that overlooked the grounds. They watched the dinosaurs mingle and graze. Laura recalled the past few hours. She had sent the mother raptor on ahead, signing that she should take them back to the sanctuary. The mother raptor understood and left with her new pack. She and Bradley had left shortly after, stopping occasionally to enjoy the beautiful scenery and each other. Now, as she sat here something puzzled her. Why didn't the female Nanotyrannus kill her? Why was she still alive?

"I see the Raptors are settling in nicely." Bradley stated. "To bad they can't stay here."

"Ya, too bad."

Bradley looked at his wife, noting her aloof nature. "I see you are still puzzling over the Nano not killing you. Personally, I am glad the mother raptor was with you. I owe her one."

"I agree with you on that. Well I just can't think of the reason so I am going to bed." With that Laura got up, gave her husband a kiss good-night and walked into the bedroom.

For a moment Bradley sat watching the Raptors bring down a young Hadrosaur. 'Efficient killing machines,' he thought. He went to bed shortly after.

* * * * *

The next morning work began on preparing the Raptors for the journey to Ebony Island. There was also the task of meeting with the scientists to see what progress has been accomplished about what ailed the plant eaters. Walking into the lab located behind the house Laura was greeted with a hub-bob of activity. Five of the lab techs were scurrying about running tests and checking results. One of the scientists looked up and saw her, rushed over to greet her. He looked to be in his early forties, wearing a white lab coat over his clothes and wire frame glasses sat on a round pudgy nose. His hair was dark with slight traces of gray. Showing at that early age he would most likely be all gray by age fifty. His personality out-weighed his looks as shown in his bubbly nature in the way he greeted her.

"Mrs. Sinclair! How good of you to come. I have good news. We have found the answer to the problem for the dinosaurs. Come with me and I will show you." Walking over to a table full of loose papers, Petri dishes, and flasks he offered her a stool to sit on and he took the one next to it.

"After taking samples from the dinosaurs and running tests I decided to take a tour of the area where the sauropods roamed. I especially took note of the many piles of solid waste and how long it took them to disappear. It was obvious that the solid waste ecosystem is grossly unbalanced, especially since the animals are in an enclosed area. They are producing more solid waste than the insects can handle. They cannot keep up."

"So what type of insects are we talking about?"

"This would mostly involve the beetle."

Reaching for one of the papers he brought out a chart. "If we look at the estimated weights of the largest of the sauropods they average out to fifty-five to a hundred or more ton. This means that just one could eliminate well over a ton and a half of solid waste per day. Now, consider them as they travel in groups."

"Oh my, that is a lot of _____!"

"Exactly! Dinosaur herds had to be accompanied by thousands of these beetles. I estimate, per dung heap at least fifty to a hundred thousand of the insects should be present, but they are not. There are other insects involved as well and one of these is the Soldier Fly. The larvae eat rotting plant and animal matter very quickly. Unfortunately they are not in abundance here."

"So how can we fix this?"

"As far as you know the dinosaurs on Ebony Island were not getting sick, right?"

"Yes, none of them got sick while I was there."

"Good. I think moving the young ones to Ebony Island would help reduce the number of solid waste mounds. The adults will have to remain here. Then we could set up several Soldier Fly larvae bins to produce a working stock of larvae. When they start to produce we can take some of the larvae and place them on the mounds. Also we could incorporate more beetles to the area. Finally, when and if the adults have any young they can be brought to Ebony Island when old enough."

"This makes sense. Let's get started on this right away."

A few minutes later Laura left the lab feeling good. The knowledge that there was no contagious disease lifted her spirits so she decided to visit the Raptors. Greeting them with a soft clicking sound she approached the mother raptor. Laura quickly noticed the new nest they had constructed and the one egg it contained. She signed 'happy for you.' The mother raptor responded with soft clicking sounds. Laura smiled as the mother raptor settled on the egg to keep it warm. At that moment something clicked for Laura as the puzzle she had been trying to solve became quite clear, hitting her with the full force of its meaning. Saying a quick good-bye to the mother raptor she rushed back up to the house.

* * * * *

Bradley sat in the study working on some papers dealing with the business conference call he had just hung up from when Laura burst into the room. With her beautiful wind blown hair and her face flushed from running up the hill Bradley thought she was even more beautiful than ever before.

"I have figured it out Bradley."

"Figured out what, my dear."

"Why I am still alive. The reason the Nanos had not made a number of appearances was because they were nesting. I was to be training prey for the Nano's young hatchlings. There are babies out there!"

❈ ❈ ❈ ❈ ❈

Laura felt the easiest way to find the hatchlings, which may be as big as a juvenile now, was to go to the area where they had encountered the parents, figuring they would not hunt too far from them. Once again Laura armed herself with the backpack and her belt of knives. Since she did not know how much the hatchlings had grown she also included a dart pistol with a good supply of darts. Once she located them she would radio Bradley to bring in the cage via helicopter, similar to what JT had used to capture the male Raptor for his horrible games, although this time it would be used to help and not hurt.

By late afternoon she was ready to leave. The mother raptor was ready as well. The alpha male would stay with the egg and keep the five young ones in line. The two, once again set out, this time with a distinct direction in mind.

A while later they arrived at the first clearing. They searched the surrounding foliage, having no success. Moving to the second clearing they expanded the search and found what they were seeking. Fifty yards from the clearing, secluded under a grove of trees was the nest. Looking inside Laura could see two baby Nanos, each a bit bigger than a juvenile Velociraptor, which made them equivalent to a medium size dog. The nest itself was deeper, at least four feet whereas the Raptors were only two feet.

The two Nanos were quiet until they heard Laura and the mother raptor above them. Then there was the symphony sound of two very hungry babies. Laura turned to the mother raptor and signed, 'Can you get them something to eat from the carcasses.' The mother raptor made a harrumph sound and left. Laura knew she wasn't too thrilled about helping the young of her enemies.

A few minutes later she returned and regurgitated over the nest. The young ones jumped on it immediately. The mother raptor left to return with more. She did that one more time, then waited.

After they finished the two looked up at them, acting as though they wanted more. It had been some time since they had last eaten, but the mother raptor would get no more. She most likely knew what enough for them was.

Reaching into her backpack Laura brought out the dart gun. The mother raptor saw it and backed up a step, remembering the last time she saw one. Setting the gun on the ground Laura reassured the mother raptor that it will be alright and the gun would not be used on her. Laura picked the gun back up and, checking the darts for the proper dosage, aimed it at the baby Nanos and fired. A few minutes later they were asleep.

Crawling into the nest Laura picked each one up and placed them in the grass, outside the nest. She checked each one to see that they were breathing all right. Once she was satisfied Laura turned to the mother raptor and signed, 'Can you take one gently and place in center of clearing?' The mother raptor lifted her lip slightly and snorted. Laura looked at her friend and smiled. 'You naughty girl!' she signed. 'Remember, you are going to be a mother soon.'

The mother raptor clicked softly and nudged Laura in play. Laura laughed, rubbing her friend's neck. "Come on girl, let's get going."

Carefully each one picked up a young Nano, Laura using her arms, the mother raptor, using her powerful jaws. When they reached the clearing they walked to its center and placed each one in the grass. She looked at them as they slept. They would be out for a good hour yet.

Removing the radio from her backpack she put a call through to her husband. When finished she placed it back in her pack. While doing so her eyes strayed to the carcasses a few feet away. Laura frowned. Something did not look right with them. Walking a bit closer she could see something was terribly wrong. Both carcasses had no head, each being removed with quick precision. Suddenly Laura felt very cold inside as she realized what it told her—Poachers!

She quickly retrieved her radio only to have it fly out of her hand in hundreds of pieces, causing her to jump. Just then another shot followed the first and she turned in time to see the mother raptor fall to the ground. She screamed. Quickly she ran toward the mother raptor only to be stopped short by another gun shot that tore up the ground beneath her feet. It was then she saw the two men walking toward her. Suddenly she wished she was facing another dinosaur.

"Look what we got here Jim."

Both men looked dirty, their faces unshaved. Each wore a type of camouflage clothing, jeans, boots, and shoes and was heavily armed. Laura guessed Jim's height at five feet, ten inches whereas his partner was a bit taller. It was also evident they were in no way overweight, each showing themselves to be in good shape, possibly due to walking so many miles.

"Ya Billy, I think we hit the jackpot. Look at this Velociraptor. I told you it pays to listen to the news. We should get a good amount for her." With that he took out one of his carving knives and moved toward the mother raptor.

Laura screamed, "Don't you touch her!"

Before they knew what she was doing she took one of her dart knives from her belt and threw it at Jim, hitting him in the arm and causing him to drop his knife, yelping in pain.

"Why you little bitch," cried Billy as he walked over to her and back-handed her across the face, knocking her to the ground. Bending over her he reached down and cut the belt from her waist.

Laura pushed herself up to a sitting position. She scowled at him as she wiped the blood from the corner of her mouth. When she placed her hand back on the ground to help push herself to her feet she felt something cold and hard. Feeling for its shape she realized it was the dart gun. It had fallen out of her backpack.

"I think we better check that backpack too," stated Jim as he came over, holding a blue bandanna over his arm.

With a couple of quick strokes of Billy's knife the backpack went the same way as the belt. Taking a look inside he let out a whistle. "Hoo-wee, this woman is loaded for bear." Jim came over to look and exclaimed to when he saw the other knives. "She has some really nice pieces here."

"You mean had," laughed Billy. Jim nodded in agreement.

While they were distracted Laura took a dart from her pocket, removed the safety cap and placed it in the dart gun. Taking aim she pulled the trigger. Jim's quick ouch as he slapped the side of his neck told her she was successful in hitting her mark.

"Ouch, Billy she shot meeeee," he remarked as he slumped to the ground.

Billy shot a scathing look in her direction as Laura started to load the dart gun again but Billy was to fast for her, knocking the gun out of her hand.

"It's time you learned a lesson you won't soon forget, woman." With that he threw her down as she struck out at him hitting, kicking, and screaming. He quickly pinned her as the faint sound of a helicopter reached their ears.

* * * * *

The mother raptor's eyes flickered open to see her friend was in trouble. She wanted to get up, but something was holding her back. She had to get up now. She had to fight this new threat. She also felt sleepy and shook herself to wake up, part of her body not wanting to respond. She pushed herself until she was able to stand.

* * * * *

"Damn police," shouted Billy. Getting to his feet he pulled Laura up with him. "You and I are going to get to know each other really well, but first we need to get out of sight. With that he turned to head for the trees and came face-to-face with the mother raptor.

Narrowing her eyes the mother raptor snarled and hissed at the man. Her sharp talon claws flexed as she took a step forward. Panicking Billy took Laura and pushed her at the mother raptor. Catching her balance Laura turned to see the man running for the cover of the trees so fast he almost lost his footing several times. He did not even bother to pick up his partner. So much for honor among thieves.

The sound of the helicopter grew louder and the landscape around them moved to and fro from the wind of the blades as the cage settled on the ground a few feet from them. Quickly Laura placed the two young Nanos in the cage as Bradley appeared in the doorway.

"Are you alright? I saw that man hurt you," he shouted to be heard above the sound of the chopper.

"Yes, I am alright! We have to get the mother raptor in here now. She has been shot!"

Bradley jumped into action. They soon had her resting on a soft blanket that lined the floor of the cage. Laura sat in a way that allowed the mother raptor's head to rest on her lap. Bradley signaled the pilot, twenty seconds to take off. He closed and latched the door and sat next to Laura.

As the chopper took off Laura rubbed the mother raptor's neck the way she liked as the tears streamed down Laura's cheeks. The mother raptor opened her eyes and purred softly, rubbing her head against Laura, wondering why she was sad. Laura smiled weakly, then signed, 'Love you, my friend forever.' The mother raptor purred again in response then closed her eyes to never open them again. Bradley held his wife close as the sobs racked her body.

* * * * *

A few days later, after the mother raptor's funeral they were ready to depart for Ebony Island. As they left Laura and Bradley said good-bye to Bradley's Sanctuary, making plans to come back each year as a family. She knew her son would enjoy it here. The two baby Nanos would remain at the Sanctuary in a secluded area where they could run free until they were old enough to fend for themselves; then they would be released on the other side of Ebony Island.

It had been a difficult past few days for Laura, trying to help the alpha male to understand what had happened, the burial of her friend, and the new knowledge of finding out the mother raptor would have been alive today if she had not moved to save her. Her devotion to Laura and the sacrifice she gave was too overwhelming.

The journey was uneventful, and it seemed like it had only been a few hours when it's taken two days and they were docked at Ebony Island's harbor. Bradley put the ramp down that joined the boat to the wharf. The five young Raptors were the first to leave, some using the ramp and others jumping from the boat to the wharf. One of the five jumped wrong, landing with a splash in the water. He quickly swam ashore and was greeted by an irate alpha male who chewed him out for being so careless. After telling the five to wait the alpha male went back on board to retrieve his egg. All the while, Laura and Bradley watched the proceedings. Once the egg was retrieved the alpha male approached Laura, looked at her for a moment, and then nudged her as a pack member. Turning then he crossed the ramp and disappeared into the forest, the five young Raptors following.

* * * * *

As the alpha male followed the familiar paths to his home, he remembered running the same paths with his mate. So intent was his thoughts, he almost missed the dead body of another Raptor. Walking over to it, he looked at it closely. His inspection told him it was the one who challenged the mother raptor and exiled her. This meant there was a new alpha female.

* * * * *

A little over an hour later Laura and Bradley were ready to leave the island. The captain, who owned the vessel was agreeable to the idea as he was a bit nervous being so close to the dinosaurs. So intent was he on leaving that he was not aware of the clicking noises right away, although Laura and Bradley were immediately alerted. Not sure who was coming to greet them they had the captain move the boat away from the wharf and two to three rifles loaded and ready.

What seemed like hours but was only minutes the alpha male exited the forest, followed closely by another female Raptor. Laura could tell right away that the female Raptor was the one who helped save her and the mother raptor during their exile. As other Raptors made an appearance the young female walked, moving about with an air of authority. The alpha male followed her closely. It was quite evident to the couple they were putting on a demonstration of sorts.

When finished the two animals stood facing the boat and barked in unison.

Laura was impressed and honored. She signed, 'Very well done. Thank you!' The two barked again. As the boat began to move slowly away Laura gave them one last message. 'Love you both!' They understood that word, that it was a deep care word. They purred in response, rubbing against each other, then looked again at Laura and barked.

As the boat moved further away Laura watched the new monarch. The mother raptor's memory would live on, not only in her heart and mind, but in her offspring as well. Hugging each other Laura and Bradley watched Ebony Island until they could see it no more.

EPILOGUE

The young Nanotyrannus woke up from his nap with the tantalizing aroma of a new scent. It had been over twenty-four hours since he had last eaten. Since climbing out of the nest and exploring a bit he had become disoriented, not able to find his way back to the nest. Now he had a new direction. Traveling toward it the scent was almost overpowered by the scent of decaying meat. Passing by the two carcasses he found the source, fresh blood.

Jim shook himself awake from the drug of the dart gun when he felt a heavy weight on his chest. He tried to shake it off or move his arms to push it away, but he could barely move them. When his eyes opened, he gasped at the site of the dinosaur looking at him quizzically, and then watching in comical horror as the jaws opened to see sharp serrated teeth move toward him. He screamed!

ACKNOWLEDGEMENT

During the time it took me to write this publication I have had the need to conduct research. Because of this I had to contact some people. For that I dedicate this page to them.

First on my list is Mr. Will Harrison, the technical support analyst for CLS America, Inc., the worldwide leader of satellite-based environmental data collection and location and ocean operations. Thank you very much for taking the time from your busy schedule to answer my question via email. (http://www.clsamerica.com)

Number two on my list is the San Diego International Airport and those who work in the Customer Service Department, specifically the one who answered a couple of questions I had sent. I appreciate the time you took to respond, thank you very much, and the information was very helpful.

The third and most influential in my research is the San Diego Police Department in California, specifically the three main areas within, the Western Division, Central Division, and ABLE (Air Borne Law Enforcement), San Diego's own Air Support Unit. Within these three divisions are some wonderful people. From the Western Division, Officer Fenella (Kelly) Custer, thank you for putting up with me and my sometimes unending questions. Add to that is Officer Bill Farrar who also took the time from his busy schedule to talk to me on the phone. I appreciated that very much. You both helped me by putting me into an area I have never been in before. Through your eyes and knowledge I was able to go to a part of San Diego, California. Another person who helped in this was Officer Kevin Means, one of two sergeants in charge of ABLE, thank you for helping me to "get into a helicopter and take off" when I have never been in one before by answering some questions about them. Please note, if for some reason I did not describe something the right way or miss-represented something in the translation it is not your fault but mine.

APPENDIX ONE
MAPS

Observation Room

maintenance
door to arena

viewing window

entrance
and exit
to lobby

selected guests seating

cage floor to ceiling

mother raptor

Bradley

cot

to rest room

Ebony Island

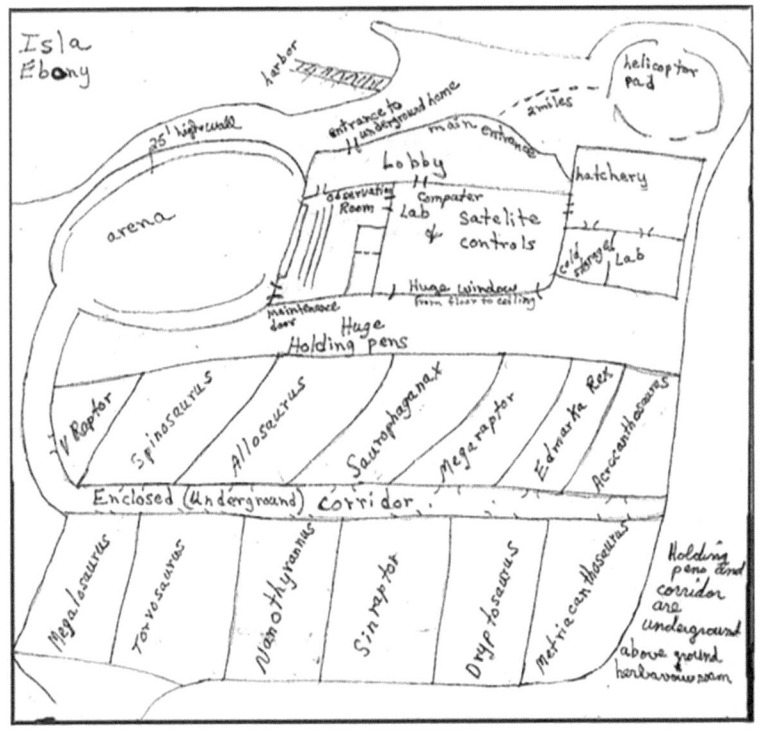

APPENDIX TWO
EDUCATIONAL DINOSAUR GLOSSARY

This is a condensed list of the dinosaurs used in this book. If you want the complete glossary please email me at **purring_tiger2000@yahoo.com** and I will send as a PDF file.

In the subject line put "requesting glossary". The complete glossary has images to give you, the reader a general idea of the animals portrayed while reading so as to gain a better visual of the events set throughout.

Theropods (meat-eaters)

Allosaurus
Length: 35ft
Height: 16.5 ft
Weight: 4 tons

Acrocanthosaurus
Pronounced: ak-ro-KANTH-uh-sawr-us
Length: 40 ft
Height: 18 ft
Weight: 2.65 tons

Dryptosaurus
Length: 22 ft
Height: 6 ft at hips
Weight: 1.2 tons

Edmarka Rex
Length: 35ft
Height: 14 ft
Weight: 2 tons

Megalosaurus
Length: 30 ft
Height: 10 ft
Weight: 1 ton

Megaraptor
Length: 25 to 30 ft
Height: 13 ft
Weight: 1 ton

Metriacanthosaurus
Pronounced: Met-ree-uh-Can-tho-Sore-us
Length: 23 to 26 ft
Height: 6 ft at hips 9 to 11 ft total
Weight: 1 to 2 tons

Nanotyrannus
Pronounced: nan-oh-tie-ran-us
Length: 17 ft
Height: 11 ft
Weight: 1 ton

Saurophaganax
Pronounced SORE-oh-FAGG-an-axe
Length: 40 ft to 50 ft
Height: 17 ft
Weight: 4-6 tons

Sinraptor
Length: 25ft
Height: 10 ft
Weight: 1 ton

Spinosaurus
Length: 43ft 9 in.
Height: 16 ft top of head. 19 ft 7 in. top of fin
Weight: 9 tons
Torvosaurus
Pronounced: (TORE-vow-SORE-us)
Length: 33-40 ft
Height: 8 ft at hips
Weight: 2-6 tons

T-Rex
Pronounced: "Tie-RAN-uh-sore-us rex"
Length: 40 ft
Height: 15-20 ft
Weight: 5-7 tons

Velociraptor
Length: 6ft
Height: 6-12 ft
Weight: 100-200 lbs

Sauropods (Plant-eaters)

Brachiosaurus

Diplodocus

Hadrosaurs

Mussaurus
Pronounced: moos-SORE-us

Pentaceratops

Stegosaurus
Pronounced (steg-oh-saw-rus)

Titanosaurus

Triceratops

Othnielia
Pronounced (oth-NEE-lee-ah)